Interwoven

With contributions by

Tord Boontje

Ronan & Erwan Bouroullec

Thomas Demand

Olafur Eliasson

Denise Hagströmer

Hettie Judah

Sevil Peach

Matt Price

Zoë Ryan

Peter Saville

Joël Tettamanti

Jane Withers

Interwoven

Kvadrat textile and design

Prestel

Munich · London · New York

Contents

Peter Saville
Foreword

In 2004, two Danish gentlemen appeared at my studio with a copy of the catalogue from my retrospective exhibition at the Design Museum. One was Anders Byriel, the CEO of Kvadrat; the other was his then head of communications. I didn't know them, but they knew me – and they seemed well informed.

They had decided that the evolution of their company's new identity was something that they would like me to contribute to. Anders had given great thought to working with me. He knew what I did, and that I was not somebody who had spent the last 20 years turning out brand identities. In a way, it was less of a business-to-business relationship and more akin to that of artist and patron; there was no brief, there were no tactical objectives; but Anders wanted to work with someone whose approach he found interesting.

I think that my experience with them over the last 10 years is probably quite representative of their relationship with many of their collaborators and associates, be they designers, architects or artists. Kvadrat's choices are not random; they don't pick up on transient trends; they give a lot of consideration to a possible engagement or partnership before approaching someone, and once they show that gesture of commitment to you, they stick with it.

Anders's father Poul Byriel founded Kvadrat with Erling Rasmussen in 1968; Kvadrat initiated those early fabrics in the amazing colours that we now associate with the new wave of Scandinavian furniture design. The big stories in design history all seem quite familiar now, and I'm much more interested in some of the parallel, more niche stories; this is one of those. A lot of the holistic interior ideas that Kvadrat was working on in the 1960s and 70s seem very pertinent now, particularly in the relationship of fabric and form.

Anders's visit to my studio came in the transition period during which he and Rasmussen's daughter, Mette Bendix, were taking over the company from their fathers. My feeling was that although Kvadrat had probably been quite groovy in the 1960s and 70s, the sector changed dramatically; particularly in the 1990s, when there was an increased awareness of design that really gathered momentum. Anders wanted to reset the company in his generational image.

As I began to learn more about the organisation, I immediately wanted people to start to have some idea of who Kvadrat were and where they came from; for a majority of their audience they had an impenetrable name and a blank identity. It's not just a matter of their being Danish; they also have a rural base. Their headquarters are in Ebeltoft, which is quiet and sleepy and

charming and looks out to the sea. It's a holiday area. And 90 per cent of the company lives there. Kvadrat's headquarters are still the embodiment of its founding ideas and spirit; there's a communal atmosphere to the place, with a great big dining area and kitchen where everybody gathers for lunch together; there's very much a family feeling.

Kvadrat is still a family business, but one that is surrounded by an extended family of creative partnerships, and it is these relationships that form the heart of this book. Collaborations with designers such as Tord Boontje and the Bouroullecs have taken the company in new directions; as with Kvadrat's projects with artists such as Thomas Demand or Olafur Eliasson, they happen because there is a common sensibility, because Anders wants to facilitate their work and because he feels passionate about it. That's why I'm always evangelical about Kvadrat, because they work according to the kind of template that one idealised in the past; relationships between artist, designer and manufacturer that are driven by belief and commitment, in the way the canon of great design has always been forged.

Facing page: Léon van Roy, illustration, 1965

Olafur Eliasson and Günther Vogt
Your glacial expectations, 2012

'What struck me on my first visit to Kvadrat was the sky, and how the landscape allowed the sky to be particularly present. This part of Denmark has a quite specific geological footprint from the Ice Age. The landscape around Kvadrat is a moraine landscape: it was carved out long ago by the movement of glaciers. And not so far away is the Mols Bjerge national park, a very hilly area. So you have this hilly landscape, and particular geological traces that were formed when the glaciers retreated. In this sense, the mirrors are reminiscent of shiny glacial pools, reflecting the sky in their surfaces. I think the idea of the withdrawing ice is a beautiful concept – its reference to a past period of global warming and the changes that happen over a period that is so vast that it is hard to grasp or understand. The idea that the sky and the atmosphere are the vehicle for these large-scale developments inspired Günther Vogt and me to try to understand the incomprehensible. If humans lived for millions of years, then the withdrawal of the ice would feel like yesterday. So the idea for the landscape in Ebeltoft was to have fresh marks as if it had only just happened. The mirrors are like little puddles from the ice that just left, like when you have snow and the spring comes and you are left with puddles of melted snow for a while until they dry up. In Iceland, I have often been struck by how bold the reflections in glacial pools appear. So the idea to create these reflection pools came in resonance with the idea of bringing the general landscape back to a more geological shape. […] I felt the subtlety, the quietness, and the focus on light reflected well on the work atmosphere in the factory. I thought that such a detail would be a good starting point for an artwork integrated into the landscape.'

Olafur Eliasson
Photography by Annabel Elston

Denise Hagströmer

Introduction: Kvadrat,
collaboration and continuity

Architect-designer Mogens Koch with his wife, weaver Eva Koch

Kvadrat (Danish for 'square') emerged at the height of the 1960s frenzy for all things Scandinavian in design to instant international acclaim. Today it is a European leader in international textile production, with a back catalogue of high-profile commissions and some of the most iconic product placements worldwide. Yet at the same time it somehow seems to be the most famous Scandinavian brand that no one has ever heard of.

Mapping the path that led to this paradoxical situation takes us through the collaborations with artists, designers, craftspeople and architects that have underpinned Kvadrat's commercial success. It follows the company's development from the early entrepreneurial story of two Danish pioneers in art and design, through the increasingly significant contribution of their roles in the rise of the concept of the modern interior. Today Kvadrat is practically an institution in the world of textiles and architecture, at the same time still acting as an international art and design catalyst, yet the company's historical significance has until this point been largely unacknowledged.[1]

'We wanted to do Scandinavian design' is how Poul Byriel and Erling Rasmussen explain their intention in the early 1960s – a time of idealism and optimism in Danish design in the light of increasing international success.[2] Alongside a focus on the domestic interior,

this era also saw the rise of the so-called 'contract interior', and Danish textiles were officially seen as part of a 'vigorous expansion of exports'.[3]

But while Denmark had enjoyed a high international profile in ceramics and metalwork since the early twentieth century, and Danish furniture had gained increasing international fame from the interwar years onwards, prior to World War II Denmark was an importer, not an exporter, of textiles.

Denmark's textile-design industry was, then, a comparatively late starter, and in 1961 was even simplistically referred to as 'in many respects a decidedly new creation.'[4] It is significant that the fledgling Danish textile-design industry distinguished itself, not least in relation to its Nordic neighbours, by pioneering collaborations between architect-designers and textile artist-designers.[5]

Following wartime rationing and shortages of materials, it was initially the architect-designers who sought improved collaboration between hand-weavers and industry and spelt out how production of their upholstery fabrics should reach modern furniture industry standards. Among them was Mogens Koch, who had worked with the influential furniture architect-designer Kaare Klint and took the following view: 'The hand-weaver was to produce a fabric with such a

personal aura that it could be produced by machine without losing its artistic integrity, while the manufacturer for his part was to show respect for the hand-weaver's wishes with regard to colours and materials.'[6]

At the historical core of this strategy were the basic principles of the international Arts and Crafts movement: 'that the fine and applied arts were equals', and its 'guiding concept of noble simplicity' – ideals which had in turn fuelled the international modern movement and were apparent in its 'machine aesthetic' and social commitment.[7]

From a background in fine art and ceramics, Lis Ahlmann went on to become a master weaver and was regarded as the pioneer 'functionalist' (as proponents of the modern movement are known in Denmark) in domestic textiles. Encouraged by Kaare Klint (originally her tutor) to rediscover historic techniques of Danish vernacular textiles, Ahlmann's fusion of history and modernity was described by Mogens Koch in 1944 as '… using as a basis the discoveries made in Danish weaving art (vævekunst) of the past … she has cultivated these and renewed the art of weaving, always with a simple, clean technique.'[8]

This was a time of growing demand from an increasingly design-conscious furniture industry for large-scale innovative textile production. Answering

Finn Juhl, *Trusteeship Council Chamber*, UN Building, New York, 1947–1950
Facing page: Poul Byriel and Erling Rasmussen with a client at the Kvadrat showroom, Adelgade, c.1970

Interior at the Cabinetmakers' Guild furniture exhibition, Copenhagen, 1958. Interior and furniture designed by Børge Mogensen, made by Erhard Rasmussen with upholstery designed by Lis Ahlmann.

this demand, Lis Ahlmann, working with architect-designer Børge Mogensen (also a former student of Klint's) from 1953, blazed a new trail in design development, joining forces with the C. Olesen textile company in 1956 to create the Cotil (CO[lesen tex]TIL) committee with the intention of raising standards in domestic textiles.[9] Unique prototypes were developed and materials and techniques were selected for commercial viability and adapted for machine production. Work by numerous craft weavers and printmakers was put into large-scale production with conspicuous success, both nationally and internationally. Kvadrat's production was based on similarly fruitful methods of collaboration, and the Designmuseum Danmark collection today includes hand-woven Kvadrat prototypes used as the basis for machine production of classic designs.[10]

Architect-inspired furniture fabrics became part of an ensemble in which textiles and wood combined to produce a characteristic element of modern interior design. Paula Trock, among others, worked with Unika Væv, founded to supply the demands of modernism in 1946 by polymath artist, entrepreneur and facilitator Baron Percy von Halling-Koch (nicknamed 'Bum'). For the prototypical modernist signifier of panoramic glazing, Trock developed a sophisticated transparent curtain fabric that filtered and scattered light to create

a cool, neutral design environment. It was used in the *Trusteeship Council Chamber* at the UN Building, New York, designed by Finn Juhl (1947–1950).[11]

The success of this collaboration between craft, design and commerce was later noted by British textile historian Mary Schoeser: 'The Scandinavian recognition of the importance of the relationship between fabric and furniture is nowhere better illustrated than by the example of Børge Mogensen's 1945 [*Spoke-back*] sofa, which did not sell until 1963, when fabric from a prototype by the Danish weaver Lis Ahlmann was developed for use with it.'[12]

Machine-woven textiles for interior decoration were not the only successful fabrics produced in postwar Denmark. Fabrics in which pattern was highlighted as a decorative feature in modern home furnishing typified textiles' contribution to the postwar 'Danish Modern' and 'Danish Design' concepts.[13] With furniture being such a central theme in Danish design production, Kvadrat's significance to the Danish furniture industry did not go unnoticed.

Official recognition of Kvadrat's achievements came when the company garnered the Møbelprisen 87 for their 'courage and sensibility in modern domestic culture', presented by the Danish furniture manufacturer's association.[14] Extracts from the award ceremony speeches reveal how Kvadrat were perceived by the furniture industry after some two decades of joint enterprise: 'With great success, their work has furthered Danish textile tradition – a tradition created by people such as Kaare Klint, Mogens Koch, Børge Mogensen and Lis Ahlmann and her students'.[15] The mention of these names together was no coincidence. The jury continued: 'By inviting contemporary textile artists to collaborate in the design of a diversity of domestic textiles, Kvadrat has positioned itself as a direct extension of this lineage … its fabrics are modern, in the best sense of the word, having contributed to shaping today's image of Danish domestic culture, and with it, Danish furniture.'[16]

In response, and with characteristic humour, Kvadrat's Poul Byriel and Erling Rasmussen expressed their pleasure in receiving the award, saying, 'It is always a good feeling to experience that your affection is reciprocated.'[17] Having acknowledged the 'very fruitful and rewarding' collaboration with the furniture association's members, they then added 'particularly the experimental and design-orientated manufacturers, and not least their affiliated [furniture] architect-designers.'[18] Besides the names the jury mentioned, Byriel and Rasmussen went on to acknowledge those to whom they owed the most. 'We have probably felt

Nanna and Jørgen Ditzel, *Floating Dock* modular seating stysten, 1961 (produced by Poul Kolds Savværk)

most connected to those in the business who are experimental and internationally orientated,' they said, 'which we find in [the architect-designers] Arne Jacobsen, Finn Juhl, Grete Jalk and Verner Panton, to mention only a few. As for textiles, we feel as if we are a child of Percy von Halling-Koch and his work at Unika Væv – and its designers, including Professor Aagaard Andersen, Nanna Ditzel and Verner Panton, for whom he [Halling-Koch] was an instigator.'[19] This roll call of luminaries from the fine-art, furniture and textile-design avant-garde underscores Kvadrat's visionary outlook. All were multidisciplinary, in particular Panton, whose exhibitions and displays Byriel had previously helped build.[20] As for Unika Væv, at a time of crisis in Danish textile production in 1952, it had demonstrated the way forward by initiating a shift in production and sales from hand-woven to machine-woven textiles.[21]

Byriel and Rasmussen continued, 'Their inspiration and experience has not only given us an exciting and personal acquaintance with Danish and international designers, but has also been one of the reasons for which we are today so well received – not just in Denmark, but around the world.'[22] The international success of the Scandinavian design phenomenon had itself provided an opportunity and an incentive for the Kvadrat founders.

This concept of 'light, modest and functional' design was internationally mediated by Scandinavian design reform organisations from the early 1950s to the late 1960s, reaching literally millions across the Western world. The Scandinavian Design label, effectively promulgated for purposes of trade and international public relations, first appeared in the title of the 1951 *Scandinavian Design for Living* exhibition at Heal's department store in London. Scandinavian Design was a construction, a strategic alliance, to 'bolster strength from a co-Nordic common front'.[23] Embracing the concept of the 'modern interior', it joined the top table of international high culture, and the Danes, like other nations, to quote design historian Penny Sparke, 'used the arrival of the "designed interior" as a vehicle through which to express the distinctiveness of their modernised postwar national identities'.[24]

By the mid 1950s, however, the Italian design industry had already caught up with Scandinavia, while Britain had seen the genesis of pop design, and American, Japanese and German design were also jostling for top billing. By the 1960 *Milan Triennial Exhibition of Decorative Arts and Modern Architecture*, 'the Scandinavian hegemony was seriously shaken'.[25]

As Kvadrat benefited from the Scandinavian Design label's international reputation, Kvadrat's own reputation went from strength to strength and continued long after the (first) zenith of Scandinavian design, a situation to which its 'ideological godparent' Unika Væv and its successor the Halling-Koch Design Center had contributed.[26] For Kvadrat's founders, Byriel and Rasmussen, the Scandinavian Design phenomenon boosted their 'professional capital' and represented a design culture both would absorb from within.

'We're like Batman … we'll come flying!'

Kvadrat's founders met in the early 1950s, working at Alfred Lem's interior design shop Lems Bolighus in Aarhus, Jutland (which has been called a provincial version of the renowned Illums Bolighus in Copenhagen). Rasmussen left Lem's curtain department in 1956 to spend three years at Unika Væv, then moved to Gabriel A/S of Aalborg.[27]

After working in Lem's furniture department, Byriel also moved to Unika Væv, to take over Rasmussen's job there as salesman, at first for southern Jutland; he then spent 'instructive and memorable years' in Stockholm, covering Sweden and Finland.[28] Denmark had a longstanding admiration of Swedish and Finnish textiles; while Swedish furniture manufacturers, on the other hand, envied the impeccable feel of

Nanna Ditzel, fabric samples, Halling-Koch Design Center, 1965

Nanna Ditzel, colour sample proposals for *Hallingdal*, 1965

Nanna Ditzel and Percy von Halling-Koch in the showroom of the Halling-Koch Design Center, 1965

Nanna Ditzel, *Hallingdal* upholstery for DSB Danish National Railway, *c*.1987

craftsmanship that Danish mass-produced furniture commonly had.

In 1964, Halling-Koch left Unika Væv to set up the Percy von Halling-Koch Design Center, an independent design company at which he masterminded concept development and agreements without financial involvement in production. He then approached architect-designer Nanna Ditzel, who had been known for challenging design orthodoxy since the 1950s – 'crossing a pink with a turquoise' at a time 'when discreet green and rust brown were the wildest colours.'[29] Her eclectic collection for 1965 included rugs, furniture, curtain fabrics, blankets and men's ties, based on an equally wide-ranging palette of 36 colours and manufactured across Europe. One particularly successful part of the collection was the 70/30 per cent wool/viscose *Hallingdal* upholstery fabric (its name combining Halling-Koch's with the manufacturer's), produced by Gudbrandsdalens Uldvarefabrik in Norway.[30]

Byriel and Bent Olsen had meanwhile got together to form Kvadrat in 1962. The name was inspired by the grid pattern on the paper that designers and engineers use to sketch ideas on: 'We looked at the small square on our paper and realised its potential and decided then and there that would be our name.'[31]

In 1965 Halling-Koch was looking for a distributor, and settled on the new company his former colleagues had started.[32] The critical and commercial response was overwhelming and unexpected. *Hallingdal* laid the foundations for Kvadrat's success, and was eventually to become a woollen textile archetype.[33]

This was the era of 'designer culture', and Ditzel was one of the leaders of 'the new generation of European designers who transformed the look of the home, office and street … [they] quickly became increasingly visible … their faces and names frequently featuring in both specialised and household press'.[34] With the force of their modernist heritage behind them, Ditzel and her contemporaries 'were seen as possessing the power to improve the quality of everyday life'.[35] *Hallingdal* remains a discreet yet almost ubiquituous presence in private homes, hospitals, airports and trains; most prominently on DSB (Danish National Railways) since 1987. Ditzel continued to challenge design orthodoxy – including that of her modernist forebears – throughout her career.

Polymath artist and designer Gunnar Aagaard Andersen was a similarly iconoclastic figure on the Danish scene, of whom Halling-Koch wrote, 'It was him and his textile sculptures [of the 1950s onwards] that opened my eyes to colours and the endless possi-

bilities that lie in the variation of their values. Light and shade. Warm and cold … Never before or since have I met anyone with his ability to be inspired by a sound, a raindrop or a rhythm, then turn these impressions into an immediate visual form … his "seven clean colours plus black and white" gospel had quite an impact …'[36] This is exemplified in his highly successful *Bolivia* collection (acquired by the Designmuseum Danmark in 2011), which predates Ditzel's *Hallingdal*, and his *Letters* textile wall hanging of 1955, consisting of interleaved lines of text. It's a design that is in production today by Kvadrat as upholstery fabric. Kvadrat and the Halling-Koch Design Center continued their highly successful collaboration until 1983.

Kvadrat appeared in the midst of what has come to be called design's pop movement period: 'a spontaneous outburst of expendable forms and materials, bright colours and provocative decoration. It represented a commitment to pleasure and instantaneity', in the words of Penny Sparke.[37] One of Halling-Koch's personal discoveries at this time – and another future Kvadrat collaborator – was to become synonymous with pop. Architect-designer Verner Panton, who began as an assistant at Arne Jacobsen's studio, became a hugely influential force on the international design-cultural scene and will forever be associated with the

Gunnar Aagaard Andersen, installation view of exhibition at the Aarhus Kunstmuseum, Aarhus, Denmark, 1977

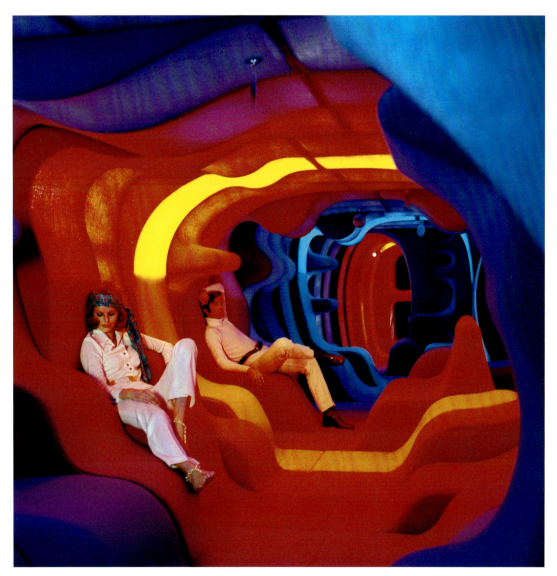

Verner Panton, *Visiona* 2, 1970 (on board the 'Lorelei' on the Rhine River, Cologne, Germany)

Above: Gunnar Aagaard Andersen, sketches and test images for *Letters*, c.1955
Facing page: Gunnar Aagaard Andersen, *Letters*, designed 1955, produced by Kvadrat 2002

Verner Panton and Percy von Halling-Koch, c.1961

Above: Léon van Roy, *We're like Batman …*, 1970 (from Kvadrat PR document)
Facing page: Léon van Roy, *Oase*, c.1970

culture of throwaway design and art, happenings and 'environments'.

The leading Danish design periodical at the time was *Mobilia*, founded in 1955 by charismatic publisher Gunnar Bratvold, who co-edited it with designer and writer Poul Henningsen and architect-designer Grete Jalk. It was published in four languages and 90 per cent of its sales were abroad. The members-only Mobilia Club, which met in the mock-medieval Eriksholm castle near Helsingør from 1963–66, provided an influential lobbying and networking forum for an international architecture, art and design cognoscenti; Byriel visited as Halling-Koch's guest.[38]

In 1967, Byriel asked Rasmussen to join him as a partner and in 1968, together with Bent Olsen (who left the company in 1977) they formed Kvadrat A/S.[39] Rasmussen took charge of administration and sales and Byriel of contact with artists and suppliers. Kvadrat's 'production' consists, in Byriel's words, of 'the idea and product development, getting these products home and selling them on.'[40] Before selling them on, however, on their arrival from weavers and printers around Europe, the fabrics were, and are, rigorously quality-controlled. The PR copy from 1970 is typically humorous: 'We're like Batman, we know everything. Write – and we'll come flying!'[41]

One collaboration that was to be of major significance to Kvadrat was with architect-designer Erik Ole Jørgensen, who, having been artistic leader at the L.M. Foght textile manufacturer, joined Kvadrat in 1971 to design their showrooms and exhibition stands. And further proof from that period of their continuing at the forefront of trends came in the form of another bestselling upholstery fabric, *Tonus*, by textile artist Nina Koppel, in 1974.

Less well known, however, are the early Kvadrat visual identity cartoons commissioned from Denmark-based Belgian artist and illustrator Léon van Roy, in a style recalling that of *Yellow Submarine* cartoonist Heinz Edelmann. Commented Halling-Koch, 'These cartoons captured the philosophy behind the product development and marketing, rather than the products' excellence.'[42] Léon, as he was known professionally, also designed op-art fabrics and rugs for Kvadrat in the early 1970s.

Kvadrat's identity is closely bound up with its geographical location, the medieval coastal village of Ebeltoft, set among the rolling hills of east Jutland – despite the fact that Kvadrat arrived there by pure chance. Kvadrat's first home was Bent Olsen's summer cottage, a former bookbinder's workshop in Femmøller, near Ebeltoft. Later they decided to locate Kvadrat's

HQ in Ebeltoft village, according to a 1966 interview 'because our wives will "keep an eye on the shop" when, for a large part of the year, we are out on sales trips.'[43] A sequence of makeshift post-agricultural bases then followed.[44]

Progress in tandem: new headquarters and national retrospective

In 1980, Kvadrat decided to build new headquarters just south of Ebeltoft, looking over Aarhus bay and the Mols Bjerge national park. The result, an understated *Gesamtkunstwerk* by architects Poulsen & Therkildsen of Aarhus, is a workplace that embodies the Kvadrat philosophy, fusing architecture and topography with art and design, and a project that attracts both national and international study visits. Lithographer Finn Sködt devised the spatial colour scheme, integrating site-specific art into the common spaces. His later commissions in textile design were a natural progression from this project. Sködt first worked for Kvadrat in the 1970s, on the company's visual identity, a role currently continued by UK art directors Peter Saville and Graphic Thought Facility.

At the inauguration of the new HQ, Halling-Koch, in keeping with his reputation for idiosyncratic PR

Top: Poulsen & Therkildsen architects, Kvadrat headquarters, Ebeltoft, 1992
Above: atrium, Kvadrat headquarters, Ebeltoft, 1992
Facing page: Erik Heide, sculpture of a raven installed at Kvadrat headquarters, Ebeltoft, 1982

Above: Finn Sködt, *Lux*, 1989
Facing page: Finn Sködt's murals in the atrium of the Kvadrat headquarters, Ebeltoft, 1982

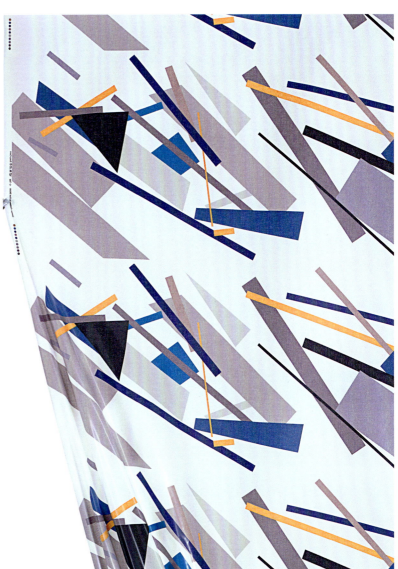

Finn Sködt, *Cursiva*, 1983

Fabric-themed tandem bicycle, presented by Percy von Halling-Koch to Byriel and Rasmussen, 1980
Facing page: Nina Koppel, *Tonus*, 1974 (*Tonus* was one of Kvadrat's first elastic woollen fabrics)

Poster by Finn Sködt for the *Kvadrat Textiles through 20 Years* retrospective at the Designmuseum Danmark, 1986

stunts, presented Byriel and Rasmussen with a fabric-themed tandem bicycle decorated with tassels and fringes. As the duo pedalled away together, Halling-Koch gave them a push, shouting, 'I've already been doing this for ages!' – an image irresistible to picture editors which proved a hit with the press and broadcast media nationwide.[45]

National critical recognition of Kvadrat's contribution to design history came in 1986 when what is now the Designmuseum Danmark staged the *Kvadrat Textiles through 20 Years* retrospective, summarizing the company's numerous collaborations with craftspeople, architect-designers, printmakers and painters.[46] Erik Ole Jørgensen's stark exhibition design of fabric pyramids and free-hanging fabric banners juxtaposed the old Kvadrat designers with the new. Nanna Ditzel's *Hallingdal*, by then updated through over 100 versions, was shown alongside upholstery fabrics by master weaver Hanne Vedel and architect-designers Bernt Petersen, Nina Koppel and textile designer Anne Birgitte Hansen. These examples of a quintessentially Nordic design ethos were themselves juxtaposed with international postmodernism in the form of Ole Kortzau's stylised printed pop designs, much used by the latest generation of Kvadrat consumers as a cheap-and-cheerful way of changing a room.

The pluralist theme was further explored with large-scale abstract-patterned textiles from painter Tom Krøjer – his first venture into textile design – and Finn Sködt's signature calligraphic style. This event's enthusiastic critical reception was presumably shared by the show's curators, as work from each of the exhibitors joined the museum's permanent collection.[47]

The Copenhagen co-operative Den Permanente continued the Kvadrat story in a concurrent exhibition covering the company's contemporary textiles and work by its collaborators. In her review of the show, national daily *Politiken*'s design critic Jonna Dwinger revealed concern at fluctuations in the market, to which, it seems, Kvadrat was immune: 'All is not as well within Danish textile manufacturing as one might wish ... When a jewel in the crown such as Cotil is on a zig-zag course, what this indicates is worrying; one must seek consolation where it is to be found, and today it is to be found at the young textile firm in Ebeltoft. Here they invest in artistic standards, advanced designers and quality.'[48] This was proved in the most flamboyant way by the first thing seen by visitors to the show: painter Niels Nedergaard's cotton textiles, with intense tropical colours inspired by the environment of his Cairo studio, and surface pattern which showed the influence of his former tutor, Gunnar

Aagaard Andersen. The mathematically precise patterns of *Musalas* and *Morabanu* at the same time showed a connection to intricate Arab ornament.

Both exhibitions attracted extensive coverage in the national press. Kvadrat has eschewed advertising, as journalistic coverage has proved to be of superior value. The company has also relied on the 'permanent exhibitions' of their products as used in auditoria, public and corporate spaces, and public and private transport, including the seats and interiors of the US presidential helicopter fleet during the Reagan and Clinton administrations.[49] In 1994 Erik Ole Jørgensen's *Malone* and *Molly* designs were chosen for the upholstery of the Eurostar Channel Tunnel trains.[50]

Kvadrat has resisted transient international trends, favouring self-instigated experiment instead. Says Byriel, 'If you want Provence idyll or Hollywood style, you can get it ... just not from us!' As the revolution of computer and information technology followed that of machine production of textiles, Kvadrat put Danish textile designer Vibeke Riisberg's dazzling computer-manipulated *Reflection* 3D pattern into production – once again to critical acclaim.

Italian-based American designer and printmaker Ross Littell was one of the first non-Scandinavians to work with Kvadrat, in the early 1980s. His highly experimen-

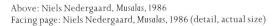

Above: Niels Nedergaard, *Musalas*, 1986
Facing page: Niels Nedergaard, *Musalas*, 1986 (detail, actual size)

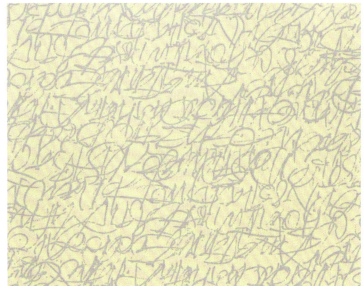

Finn Sködt, *Exlibris*, 1985

tal pieces, produced in collaboration with Finn Sködt, combined art history and geometry with technology.

Kvadrat fabric was used as a bearer of national political symbolism when British architects Foster + Partners were commissioned to design the interior of the Debating Chamber of the Bundestag in the Reichstag, along with their work on the structure of the building (1992–1999). Senior partner and head of design David Nelson explained, 'We were to create a completely new chamber; it was a unique moment in time. The fabric needed to look very good [including when the chamber was empty], have a saturated colour rich in pigment, and wear very well.'[51] And perhaps most significantly, Nelson continued, 'the fabric needed to represent a strong image of Parliament.'[52] The choice of colour was crucial: a decision that was built, interestingly, on historical continuity – a link to the chamber in Bonn. The long and complex process involved close collaboration with a keenly engaged committee representing the Reichstag. It was Parliament's wish for historical continuity that determined the choice of colour. As David Nelson has said, 'they felt they wanted to bring something with them from Bonn, that featured a different blue.'[53] Finn Sködt's cobalt-blue *Topas* soft crepe was chosen, and Danish artist-designer Per Arnoldi, adviser to Kvadrat, collaborated on the

other spaces' varying colour schemes. The Debating Chamber's seating recalls an early statement by Byriel. 'A piece of furniture', he said, 'isn't merely the piece of furniture on its own and the fabric on its own. The furniture and its upholstery should rise to a higher level.'[54] A principle which is further evinced by the longstanding relationships Kvadrat enjoys with its furniture manufacturers, which include the German maker Thonet and the Swiss company Vitra.

Further official recognition came with the Danish Design Council *Designrådet* Annual Award of 1996, for the partners' significant contribution to design development. The success of their collaboration lies in the fact that, in Byriel's words, 'we respect each other's differences and know when to be wise enough to give in.'[55] In the same year, Byriel was also the subject of a television programme examining his role as an *igangsætter* or 'creative instigator' – a distinctly Danish concept bound up with the nation's historical culture of business know-how and entrepreneurship.[56]

The direction of Kvadrat passed to the next generation in the 1990s, quite literally in the cases of the CEO – Poul Byriel's son Anders – and the product director – Rasmussen's daughter Mette Bendix. The design director is Anne Jørgensen. Following their retirement, both Poul Byriel and Erling Rasmussen continue to

maintain close links with the company; Rasmussen is also co-founder of the Ebeltoft Glass Museum.

Informing new design cultures: increased internationalisation, the global and local

Following this smooth transition, Kvadrat's corporate design culture has been conscientiously maintained alongside the company's emergence as a catalyst on the global design scene; all as part of a considered strategy to push the limits of textiles and design through developments in aesthetics, technology and art. At the same time, Anders Byriel, having 'grown up with Poul Henningsen and Verner Panton as frequent visitors', also plays an active part in the public sector, as chairman of the Danish Design Council from 2008 to 2012, and since 2013 as a member of the board of the rather lengthily named Royal Danish Academy of Fine Arts, Schools of Architecture, Design and Conservation – School of Architecture.[57]

Byriel collaborates closely with Anne Jørgensen. An interior designer by training, whose tutors were themselves taught by Finn Juhl and Børge Mogensen at the Skolen for Boligindretning (now part of the Royal Danish Academy of Fine Arts), Jørgensen first worked at the Finsk Form shop in Copenhagen, then forged an

Vibeke Riisberg, *Reflection 3D*, 1992

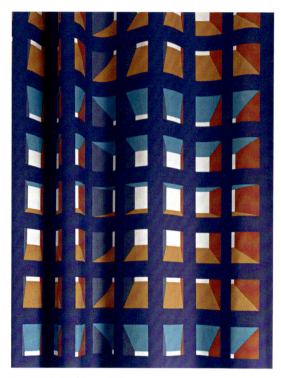

Ross Littell, *Wind Screen*, 1997
Facing page: Verner Panton, *Amoebe Highback* chair, Vitra
(designed in 1970 for the *Visiona* installation)

impressive career with the Danish furniture company Fritz Hansen (with which Kvadrat has a longstanding relationship).[58] According to Anders Byriel, she continues a colour sensibility that originated with Verner Panton and Nanna Ditzel.[59]

As an expert in how textiles affect perceptions of a space and generate atmosphere, Jørgensen explains: 'As you enter a space, rather than noticing the curtain itself, you can *feel* that somebody has been thinking about what is happening in a room.'[60] Jørgensen uses the Danish word *stemning* or 'atmosphere', with a meaning in Danish very like that of the German *Stimmung*. It conveys the sense that 'a space or room can create both an atmosphere and a mood'.[61] The use of this historically much-favoured term 'underlines the personalised, psychological qualities' of an interior.[62]

The use of textiles today, Jørgensen continues, is about small, subtle additions to convey a positive feeling: how relatively small interventions can contribute warmth, sensuality, colour and sound absorption. In respect of the latter, she remarks, 'Why […] go to a restaurant, eat nice food, and shout at each other?'[63]

Kvadrat's in-house team includes design co-ordinators, textile engineers (drafted in from over the water at the Swedish School of Textiles, Borås) and what Jørgensen calls 'master control', keeping

track of 2,500 production items. Because she believes that designers don't change their ideas on colour very much, input from around 30 freelancers at one time adds aesthetic diversity and breadth to the collection. The freelancers' backgrounds are diverse, taking in textile composition, graphic design, industrial design and architectural design. While input in this field also comes from a growing roster of international designers – including for the past several years the Italian 'colour master' Giulio Ridolfo – Jørgensen maintains, 'we still have a northern European view on colour. In Scandinavia, we take colour seriously … a grey can be many things.'[64] But what counts is not 'where the designer comes from, but what they can do' – or the quality of what Jørgensen calls the designer's 'handwriting'. Swedish textile designer Åsa Pärson's sophisticated *Missing Thread* and *M/T Colour* designs bring subtle gradations of shades of colour to public interiors, including those of Swedish embassies and the Swedish EU offices in Brussels. Displaying the same northern sensibility, her *Molly* design for Kvadrat was selected by Swedish architect-designers CKR (Mårten Claesson, Eero Koivisto and Ola Rune) for the interiors of the upmarket Nobis hotel in Stockholm.

In contrast, the *Village* curtain fabric by Argentinian-Swiss designer Alfredo Häberli uses fluorescent dye to

make a humorous point. Designed for the very specific environment of a children's hospital ward, the townscapes depicted change their appearance in twilight as hidden details are revealed in glowing colour.

Danish textile design duo Mathilde Aggebo and Julie Henriksen's approach is equally distinctive. They won public recognition for their stage curtains for the *Dronningesalen* (Queen's hall) of the Copenhagen Royal Library's *Black Diamond* extension, which featured manuscript fragments from the work of Hans Christian Andersen printed on *Divina* fabric. More recently, their collaboration with Lundgaard & Tranberg Arkitekter for the Tietgen college halls of residence in Copenhagen clearly demonstrates how textiles, graphic design, art and architecture can form a seamless whole. Aggebo and Henriksen translated the building's themes of the individual in the communal into the medium of textiles, in the process exemplifying the essential value of textiles which contribute to the whole the properties of sensuality, tactility and warmth, alongside atmosphere (Jørgensen's *stemning*). Five thousand metres of *Florentijn* in specially developed colourways form a series of prominent vertical stripes differentiating one room from another (of the 360 in total). These textiles also mark out the building's exterior, adorning the floor-to-ceiling windows with a colourful and

Above: Aggebo and Henriksen, interior and *Florentijn* fabric design, Tietgen halls of residence, Copenhagen, 2006
Facing page: Norway Says and Per Bjørnsen, *Coda* 2, 2013

ever-changing rhythmic pattern that is constantly varied as curtains are opened and drawn.

Other northern Europeans collaborating with Kvadrat include Finnish textile designer Satu Montanari, who builds on a distinctively Finnish design ethos using the extensive palette of the recently updated cotton *Pause* collection. Although the internationally orientated *Norway Says* trio of industrial designers Andreas Engesvik, Torbjørn Anderssen and Espen Voll split up in 2009, the latter two have continued the collaboration with Kvadrat, in the *Coda* 2 upholstery design.

Collections such as these are the end product of extensive collaboration – what Jørgensen calls a 'meeting process', with the designer.[65]

'We collaborate with those with whom we can
see the possibility of growing together.'

When selecting a fabric sample from a set of proposals, Jørgensen and the Kvadrat design team must consider how it will translate into the final textile.[66] They look for suppliers that can collaborate with them in developing something new,[67] they identify appropriate colourways and try to assess how well the small, handwoven sample will survive the transition into a finished textile.[68] Kvadrat collaborates with those designers with

whom they can see a possibility of growing together; Jørgensen describes the ongoing relationship as building up the designer's collection within 'our collection.'[69] In each successful case, Kvadrat orders 300m of fabric from the manufacturer. Kvadrat makes royalty payments to the designer each month, based on volume of sales. 'If it's a success for Kvadrat, it's also a success for the designer,' says Jørgensen.[70]

An insight into the artist-designer's role in this product-development process is offered by Dutch master weaver Frans Dijkmeijer, one of the first non-Scandinavians to work with Kvadrat. Interviewed in 2011 following nearly 20 years of collaboration with the company, after producing a thick file of designs and proofs that resulted in the production of one textile, he commented feelingly on just how much work it was getting textiles added to a collection.[71] He himself could sense the moment when he'd produced something with potential, however; 'Often you *feel* it. Once you're behind the loom, you realise it's new. Sometimes you work on something for months, when suddenly … You sense you've got it right.'[72] Dijkmeijer's remarkably successful output, which could be characterised as a personal take on northern European modernism, appears at first glance a simple and logical development of that tradition; but closer inspection reveals that it

has been achieved by the use of extremely complex and subtle weaving techniques. This is clearly evident in his *Vale, Ripple* and *Colline* 3D structured designs.

Danish textile designer Vibeke Riisberg, at the Kolding School of Design, Denmark, conducts in-depth research of a different kind. Kvadrat co-funded two experimental research projects at the school between 2008 and 2011, both of which indicate possible future applications; one examined how decorative textiles can be used to control interior daylight levels and reduce overheating from solar gain in office buildings; the other, how textile qualities can improve the hospital environment.[73]

Kvadrat's architectural textiles are further proof of how textiles and the modern interior can work together to mutual benefit. *Soft Cells* combines aluminium panels and tensioned textiles used as sustainable building components to improve acoustics, as installed in Foster + Partners' London architectural studio. Both the *North Tiles* and *Clouds* designs developed by French designers Ronan & Erwan Bouroullec consist of a system of textile tiles that slot together to create or divide space, contributing colour, texture and soundproofing.

Kvadrat's twenty-first-century collaborations also include their own showrooms across the world, each of which is by a different designer or architect, and

Soft Cells installed at Foster + Partners' studio, London
Facing page: Ronan & Erwan Bouroullec, *North Tiles*, 2006

where individual creativity transcends corporate style. Besides Ronan & Erwan Bouroullec's Stockholm and Copenhagen showrooms, these include flagship showrooms in Milan by Alfredo Häberli and in London by designer Peter Saville and architect David Adjaye. Similarly for Kvadrat's art projects, discussed elsewhere in this book, the only requirement is that the work involves textiles and investigates their use.

As for Kvadrat's ideological godparent, in a TV documentary on Percy von Halling-Koch, *Selling is an Art* (En sælgers liv), shown in Denmark in 1980 and Sweden the following year, Halling-Koch advised, 'With talented artists behind you, you can go out into the world and sell'. As for how this should happen, he added, 'textiles should be beautifully *shown*, not just displayed.'[74] And as predicted by Halling-Koch himself and Nanna Ditzel – currently being rediscovered by a new design generation – ideas explored by shows in commercial spaces and museums by increasingly multidisciplinary consultant designers have engendered new collaborations, and acted as important stimuli for the company down the years.[75]

Nearly 50 years after Poul Byriel and Erling Rasmussen chose it as the symbol for their new company, Frans Dijkmeijer gave an inspired analysis of Kvadrat's square: on squared graph paper, he pencilled in four squares which he then used to illustrate a 'plain weave' – 'the smallest repeat possible in the art of weaving', and then pointed out that Kvadrat had 'compressed this even further, taking it to the sublime'.[76]

Under the leadership of Byriel and Bendix, Kvadrat's revenue since 1998 has more than quadrupled, with only one other major contender operating in the same field in the world.[77] While Byriel insists there remains 'something Scandinavian in our values', a shift of perspective has nonetheless taken place: from that of a Scandinavian business to that of a European business with a global outlook.[78] Sociologist Anthony Giddens offers an apposite definition of globalisation as: 'an intensification of worldwide social relations which link distant localities in such a way that local happenings are shaped by events occurring many miles away and vice versa'.[79] Globalisation, paradoxically, facilitates diversity, and that paradox is expressed as 'glocalisation', a process Anders Byriel characterises thus: 'We realised that we've got more in common with a Japanese retailer or German architect than we have with Mr Hansen down the street in Denmark.'[80]

It is against such a complex backdrop that the jewel in the crown so far of all Kvadrat's collaborations is in Ebeltoft – part, in fact, of the physical presence of Ebeltoft itself: Danish-Icelandic artist Olafur Eliasson's large-scale landscape installation *Your glacial expectations*, created in association with Liechtenstein landscape architect Günther Vogt. In keeping with Kvadrat's carefully nurtured corporate culture, this creates aesthetic and cultural benefits for employees, locals and visitors alike, quite literally on the doorstep of the company HQ. It stands, in fact, as living testimony to the fruits of Kvadrat's tradition of creative, professional collaboration.

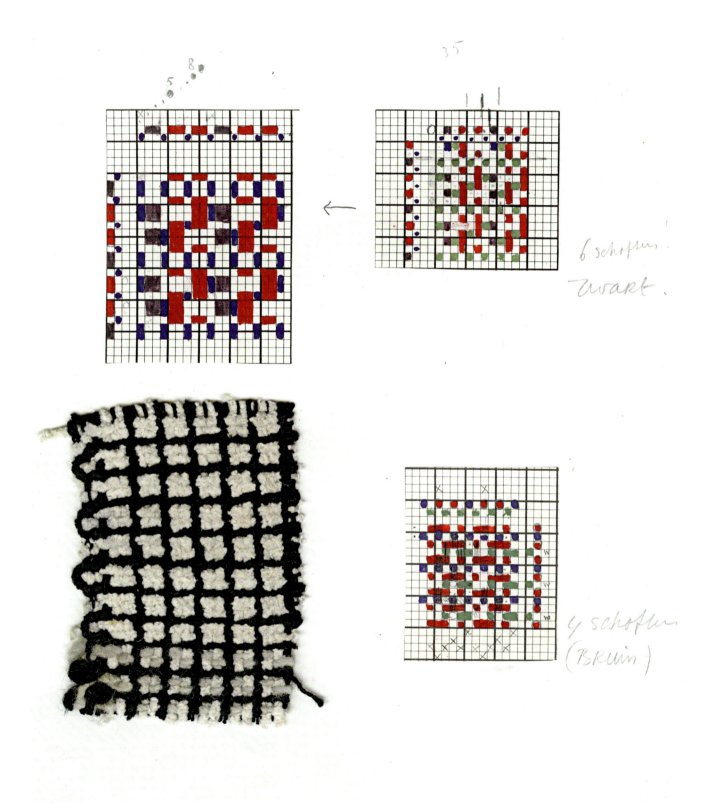

Above: Frans Dijkmeijer, sample and design showing the square grid of the weave
Facing page: Frans Dijkmeijer, *Perla* 2.2, 2012

1   I would like to thank Dorthe Aagaard Adamsen, Camilla Vissing
    Mogensen and Alice Rasmussen at Kvadrat's HQ in Ebeltoft for making
    the Kvadrat company archive available to me. Profuse thanks also to
    Anja Lollesgaard, Lars Dybdahl and Kirsten Toftegaard at the Design-
    museum Danmark, and art historian Vibeke Petersen for advice in
    relation to artist Gunnar Aagard Andersen. In writing this essay I am
    indebted to Robert Connolly for language editing.
2   Poul Byriel and Erling Rasmussen, in interview with the author,
    22 March 2012, Kvadrat HQ, Ebeltoft, Denmark.
3   Karlsen, Arne & Bent Salicath, *Moderne Dänische Textilien* [Copenhagen,
    1961], p. 5.
4   Hård af Segerstad, *Ulf, Scandinavian Design* [Nordisk Rotogravyr,
    Stockholm, 1961], p. 71.
5   Traditionally, in Scandinavia, furniture designers or 'furniture
    architects' (Swedish: *möbelarkitekt*) or 'interior architects'
    (Swedish: *inrednins-arkitekt*) have considerable spatial design or
    'interior architecture' training, hence the term 'architect-designer'.
6   Paludan, Charlotte, *The Art of Weaving. Danish Hand Weaving in the
    20th Century* [catalogue, The Danish Museum of Decorative Art,
    Copenhagen, 2004], p. 25.
7   Schoeser, Mary, *World Textiles. A Concise History* [Thames & Hudson,
    London, 2003], p. 194.
8   Sten Møller, Viggo, *Dansk kunstindustri 1900–1950* (Danish art industry
    1900–1950) [Rhodos, Bind 2, Copenhagen, 1970], p. 162.
9   Paludan, p. 25. Bent Salicath, director of the design reform
    organisation Landsforeningen Dansk Kunsthændværk, was also
    a committee member.
10 Paludan, p. 26.
11 Paludan, p. 126.
12 Schoeser, Mary, *Fabrics and Wallpapers* [Bell & Hyman, London, 1986],
    p. 63.
13 For 'Danish Design' and 'Danish Modern', see: Dybdahl, Lars (ed.),
    Dansk Design 1910–1945: Art Déco & Funktionalisme [Det Danske Kunstin-
    dustrimuseum, Copenhagen, 1997]; Dybdahl, Lars & Bruun, Mette
    (ed.), *De Industrielle Ikoner: Design Danmark,* [Det Danske Kunstindustri-
    museum (English translation by John Irons), Copenhagen, 2004]; and
    Dybdahl, Lars, *Dansk Design 1945–1975: Produktdesign : Grafisk Design :*

Møbeldesign [Borgen, Copenhagen Valby, 2006].
14 Press release, *Møbelfabrikantforeningen Pressemedelelse* (Danish
    Furniture Manufacturers' Association), 21 April 1987, Kvadrat HQ
    archive, Ebeltoft.
15 ibid.
16 ibid.
17 Document, *Tale ved prisoverrækkelsen af møbelprisen 87* (Speech at
    the Møbelprisen 87 award ceremony), Kvadrat HQ archive, Ebeltoft.
18 ibid.
19 ibid.
20 Poul Byriel, in interview with the author, 22 March 2012, Kvadrat HQ,
    Ebeltoft.
21 Document, minutes from a Unika Væv meeting, including statement
    made by Percy von Halling-Koch, January 1963, Kvadrat archive,
    Ebeltoft.
22 Document, *Tale ved prisoverrækkelsen af Møbelprisen 87* (Speech at the
    Møbelprisen 87 award ceremony), Kvadrat HQ archive, Ebeltoft.
23 Huldt, Åke H. & Laurén, Per A. (ed.), *Design in Scandinavia: USA–Canada
    1954–1957* [Svenska slöjdföreningen, Stockholm, 1958].
    See also: Hagströmer, Denise, 'An "Experiment's" Indian Summer –
    The Formes Scandinaves Exhibition 1958–1959', pp. 93–99 in:
    W. Halén, K. Wickman (eds.), *Scandinavian Design Beyond The Myth –
    Fifty Years of Scandinavian Design* [Nordiska Ministerrådet/Arvinius
    förlag, Stockholm, 2003, 2006].
24 Sparke, Penny, *The Modern Interior* [Reaktion, London, 2008], p. 197.
25 Sandström, Sven & Widman, Dag (eds.), *Konsten I Sverige. Konsthantverk,
    konstindustri, design 1895–1975* [AWE/Geber, Stockholm, 1975], p. 109.
26 For Unika Væv, see: Sieck, Frederik, ed *Bogen om Bum – Galskabens
    Triumf* (*The Book on Bum – the Triumph of Madness*) [Kvadrat, 1984] and
    Toftegaard, Kirsten, *Hallingdal 65* [International Contemporary
    Furniture Fair, Kvadrat, New York, 2012].
27 Poul Byriel and Erling Rasmussen, in interview with the author,
    22 March 2012, Kvadrat HQ, Ebeltoft.
28 ibid.
29 Undated news item cutting, Kvadrat archive, Ebeltoft.
    For more on Nanna Ditzel, see: Møller, Henrik Sten, *Bevægelse og
    skønhed bogen om Nanna Ditzel* (*Movement and Beauty: The Book on

Nanna Ditzel) [Rhodos, Copenhagen, 1998].
30 Regarding the manufacture of Hallingdal, Kirsten Toftegaard
    writes: 'What is completely out of the ordinary in Gudbrandsdalens
    Uldvarufa- brik is that both at the time and still today the factory itself
    carries out all the steps in the process, from treating the shorn-off wool,
    through the dyeing, spinning, weaving and finishing of the woven
    material. … [This complete process] is rarely seen today, now that
    firms have become fewer in number but larger and more specialised'.
    Toftegaard, Kirsten *Hallingdal 65*, 2012, p. 165. See also: *Gudbrandsdalens
    Uldvarefabrik AS 1887–2012*, 125th Anniversary Magazine, company PR
    publication, 2012.
31 Poul Byriel, in interview with Carsten Fischer, in the *Igangsætterne* televi-
    sion programme, broadcast on Danish National Television, DR, Kanal 1,
    4 July 1996, DR Archive and Research Center, Copenhagen.
32 Prior to Kvadrat, Gabriel in Fredericia were approached, but they
    rejected Hallingdal. See: Sieck, Frederik, ed, *Bogen om Bum – Galskabens
    Triumf* [Kvadrat, 1984], p. 50.
33 In 2001, Kvadrat was awarded the Danish Design Center's Classics Prize
    for Hallingdal.
34 Sparke, 2013, p. 145.
35 ibid.
36 Sieck, Frederik (ed.), *Bogen om Bum – galskabens triumf* [Kvadrat, 1984]
    p. 10. Aagaard Andersen's *Letters* upholstery fabric was relaunched in
    2002. A major exhibition, *The Lifework of Gunnar Aagaard Andersen*, curated
    by Jørgen Michaelsen and Vibeke Petersen, will take place at Den Frie
    Center of Contemporary Art, Copenhagen, from 17 August – 6 October
    2013. Vibeke Petersen's book on Aagaard Andersen is planned to be
    published in 2014.
37 Sparke, 2013, p. 170.
38 Poul Byriel, in interview with the author, 22 March 2012, Kvadrat
    HQ, Ebeltoft. See also Sieck, 1984.
39 For further information on Bent Preben Olsen, see: 'En av Kvadrats
    stiftere död' (One of Kvadrat's founders deceased), *Ebeltoft Folketidende*,
    28 September 1983, p. 18, and two items in *Århus Stiftstidende*,
    15 and 17 August 1983.
40 Danish newspaper cutting, c.1981, title missing, Kvadrat HQ
    archive, Ebeltoft.

41 c.1970, PR document, Kvadrat HQ archive, Ebeltoft. The copywriter here seems to be confusing Batman with Superman. Batman has no superpowers and cannot fly.

42 See Sieck, Frederik (ed.), *Bogen om Bum! – Galskabens Triumf* [Kvadrat, 1984].

43 Newspaper cutting, '*Boligtekstilier i tidligere rullestue*' ('Interior design textiles in former mangling room'), *Djursland* local daily 22 January 1966, Kvadrat HQ archive, Ebeltoft.

44 After Kvadrat's first HQ in Bent Olsen's summer cottage or Lines hus (1965–1967), the company moved to a former laundry mangling room in Adelgade (1967–1968), followed by a barn in Østerallé (1968–1970). Kvadrat's offices and warehouse moved to a former school in Adelgade (1970–1980), and the warehouse moved to a former dairy in Toldbodvej (1975–1980).

45 '*Makkerpar*' (lit: 'colleague couple'), *Århus Stiftstidende*, 6 September 1980, local newspaper cutting, Kvadrat HQ archive, Ebeltoft.

46 The museum's exhibition leaflet lists the exhibits as does Kvadrat's exhibition press release, dated May 1986. No curator's name is mentioned. Designmuseum Danmark Archives, Copenhagen.

47 National newspaper cutting, no title, *Politiken*, 29 May 1986, Kvadrat HQ archive, Ebeltoft.

48 Jonna Dwinger, '*Danmark i textilier*' ('Denmark in textiles'), *Politiken*, 12 May 1982, p. 9. See also, for instance, Annette Hagerup (title unclear on newspaper cutting) in *Berglinske Tidende*, 5 May 1986, Kvadrat HQ archive, Ebeltoft.

49 Local newspaper cuttings, '*Reagan satser på Kvadrat*' ('Reagan goes for Kvadrat'), *Djursland*, 16 May 1986; '*Clinton sidder på Kvadrat-stof*' ('Clinton sits on Kvadrat fabric') *Århus Stiftstidende*, 9 July 1997, Kvadrat HQ archive, Ebeltoft.

50 Local newspaper cutting, Eilertsen, Marianne, '*Kvadrat vandt tekstil-ordren til kanal-tog*' ('Kvadrat won textile order for Channel tunnel train'), *Dagbladet Djursland*, 28 June 1994, Kvadrat HQ archive, Ebeltoft.

51 David Nelson, in telephone interview with the author, 5 July 2012.

52 ibid.

53 ibid.

54 Danish newspaper cutting, c.1981, title missing, Kvadrat HQ archive, Ebeltoft.

55 Poul Byriel and Erling Rasmussen, in interview with the author, 22 March 2012.

56 *Igangsætterne* (the instigators), presented by Carsten Fischer, broadcast on Danish National Television, DR, Kanal 1, 4 July 1996, DR Archive and Research Center, Copenhagen.

57 Anders Byriel, in interview with the author, 21 March 2012, Kvadrat HQ, Ebeltoft.

58 Anne Jørgensen, in interview with the author, 21 March 2012, Kvadrat HQ, Ebeltoft.

59 Anders Byriel, in interview with the author, 21 March 2012, Kvadrat HQ, Ebeltoft.

60 Anne Jørgensen, in interview with Marleine van der Werf, in the Kvadrat video, for the Audax Textielmuseum, Tilburg, the Netherlands, 21 March 2012. www.youtube.com/watch?v=s6DuO-jKCx

61 Muthesius, Stefan, *The Poetic Home: Designing the 19th-century Domestic Interior* [Thames & Hudson, New York, 2009], p. 172.

62 Muthesius, p. 172.

63 Anne Jørgensen, in interview with the author, 21 March 2012, Kvadrat HQ, Ebeltoft.

64 ibid.

65 ibid.

66 Anne Jørgensen, in interview with Marleine van der Werf.

67 ibid.

68 ibid.

69 ibid.

70 ibid.

71 Frans Dijkmeijer, in interview with Annemartine van Kesteren, in his home and studio, Toulouse, France, in the *A Life in Weaving* video, made by the Museum Boijmans Van Beuningen, The Netherlands, 1 June 2012. See: www.youtube.com/watch?v=6XIbllhAb6I.

72 ibid.

73 For Vibeke Riisberg's research at the Designskolen Kolding, Denmark, see the articles relating to these two research projects: *User-driven Innovation and Communication of Textile Qualities*, in collaboration with Danmarks Tekniske Universitet, DTU, Danmarks Designskole, Kvadrat and Trevira-Neckelmann, 2008–2011, funded by the Danish Enterprise and Construction Authority's programme for user-driven innovation. www.designskolenkolding.dk/index.php?id=2845, downloaded 4 July 2012. See for instance: Vibeke Riisberg, Caren Weisleder and Lene Wul, 'User-driven innovation, "support-ive design", and the hospitals of the future – a new paradigm in the making?', *Design Research DK:08–09*, pp 76–83.
Secondly, *Adjusting Daylight in public buildings. Decorative textiles as a medium to adjust daylight and reduce solar heat in office buildings*, funded by the Danish Center for Design Research, the Danish Ministry of Culture's Research Pool and Kvadrat. See: www.designskolenkolding.dk/index.php?id=3429, downloaded 4 July 2012. See for instance: Joy Boutrup and Vibeke Riisberg, 'Adjusting daylight and solar heating in offices', *The Nordic Textile Journal* [vol 2, 2010], pp. 1–7, (The Textile Research Centre, CTF, Swedish School of Textiles, Borås, Sweden).

74 Percy von Halling-Koch, in interview with Hans-Georg Møller in *En Sælgers Liv* (*A Salesman's Life*), broadcast nationally in Denmark 27 February 1980 (National Library of Sweden, KB, Audiovisual Archive, Stockholm).

75 See, for instance, the large scale, international Kvadrat *Hallingdal 65* project (2012), of which Patrizia Moroso and Giulio Ridolfo were chief curators. See: hallingdal65.kvadrat.dk/designers.

76 Frans Dijkmeijer, in interview with Annemartine van Kesteren, *A Life in Weaving* video, as above.

77 See www.globaldesignforum.com/speakers/anders-byriel/

78 Anders Byriel, in panel discussion at the *Konstfack Forum in Creativity* seminar, 17 May 2008, Konstfack, National College of Art and Design, Stockholm, Sweden. See: vimeo.com/19035843

79 Franklyn, Sarah, Lury, Celia and Stacey, Jackie, *Global Nature Global Culture*, Sage, London, 2000, p. 2.

80 Anders Byriel, in panel discussion at the *Konstfack Forum in Creativity*.

Bibliography

– Aarhus Kunstmuseum and Sophienholm, *Aagaard Andersen exhibition catalogue* [Copenhagen, 1977].
– Dybdahl, Lars & Bruun, Mette (ed.), *De Industrielle Ikoner: 'Design Danmark, Det 'Danske Kunstindustrimuseum* (includes English translation), [Copenhagen, 2004].
– Franklyn, Sarah, Lury, Celia & Stacey, Jackie, *Global Nature Global Culture* [Sage, London, 2000].
– Gudbrandsdalens Uldvarefabrik AS 1887–2012, 125th Anniversary Magazine, company PR publication, 2012.
– Hagströmer, Denise, 'An "Experiment's" Indian Summer – The Formes Scandinaves Exhibition 1958–1959', in *Scandinavian Design Beyond The Myth: Fifty Years of Design from the Nordic Countries*, W. Halén, K. Wickman (eds.) [Arvinius förlag, Stockholm, 2003, 2006].
– Halén, Widar & Wickman, Kerstin (eds.), *Scandinavian Design Beyond the Myth: Fifty Years of Design from the Nordic Countries* [Arvinius förlag, Stockholm, 2003, 2006].
– Hård af Segerstad, Ulf, *Scandinavian Design* [Nordisk Rotogravyr, Stockholm, 1961].
– Karlsen, Arne & Bent Salicath, *Moderne Dänische Textilien* [Copenhagen, 1961].
– Paludan, Charlotte, *The Art of Weaving. Danish Hand Weaving in the 20th Century* [The Danish Museum of Decorative Art, Copenhagen, 2004].
– Sandström, Sven & Widman, Dag, (eds.), *Konsten I Sverige. Konsthantverk, konstindustri, design 1895–1975* [AWE/Geber, Stockholm, 1975].
– Schoeser, Mary, *Fabrics and Walllpapers* [Bell & Hyman, London, 1986].
– Schoeser, Mary, *World textiles: a concise history* [London, Thames & Hudson, London, 2003].
– Sieck, Frederik (ed.), *Bogen om Bum – Galskabens Triumf* [Kvadrat, 1984].
– Sparke, Penny, *An Introduction to Design and Culture. 1900 to the Present* [3rd edition, Routledge, London, 2013].
– Sten Møller, Viggo, *Dansk Kunstindustri 1900–1950* [Rhodos, Bind 2, Copenhagen, 1970].
– Toftegaard, Kirsten, *Hallingdal 65* [International Contemporary Furniture Fair, Kvadrat, New York, 2012].

Internet

– *User-driven innovation and communication of textile qualities*, in collaboration with Danmarks Tekniske Universitet, DTU, Danmarks Designskole, Kvadrat and Trevira-Neckelmann, 2008–2011, funded by the Danish Enterprise and Construction Authority's programme for user-driven innovation. www.designskolenkolding.dk/index.php?id=2845.
– Vibeke Riisberg, Caren Weisleder and Lene Wul, 'User–driven innovation, "supportive design", and the hospitals of the future – a new paradigm in the making?', *Design Research DK:08–09*, pp 76–83.
– *Adjusting Daylight in public buildings. Decorative textiles as a medium to adjust daylight and reduce solar heat in office buildings*, funded by the Danish Centre for Design Research, the Danish Ministry of Culture's Research Pool and Kvadrat. www.designskolenkolding.dk/index.php?id=3429.
– Joy Boutrup and Vibeke Riisberg, 'Adjusting daylight and solar heating in offices', *The Nordic Textile Journal*, 2, 2010 [The Textile Research Centre, CTF, Swedish School of Textiles, Borås, Sweden] pp. 1–7.
– *A Life in Weaving*, film about Frans Dijkmeijer, interviewed by Annemartine van Kesteren, in Dijkmeijer's home and studio, Toulouse, France, commissioned by the Museum Boijmans Van Beuningen, the Netherlands, 1 June 2012. See: www.youtube.com/watch?v=6XIbllhAb6I
– *Anne Jørgensen*, interviewed by Marleine van der Werf, for the Audax Textielmuseum, Tilburg, the Netherlands, 21 March 2012. See: www.youtube.com/watch?v=s6DuO-jKCx8.
– *Konstfack Forum in Creativity*, seminar and panel discussion including Anders Byriel, 17 May 2008, Konstfack, National College of Art and Design, Stockholm, Sweden. See: vimeo.com/19035843.

Archives

– Kvadrat HQ company archive, Ebeltoft, Denmark.
– National Library of Sweden, KB, Audiovisual Archive, Stockholm, Sweden.
– Danish National Television, DR, Archive and Research Centre, Copenhagen, Denmark.
– Designmuseum Danmark library and archive, Copenhagen, Denmark.

Television recordings

– *Igangsætterne*, on Poul Byriel, presented by Carsten Fischer, broadcast on Danish National Television, DR, Kanal 1, 4 July 1996, 21.39 – 22.13, DR Archive and Research Centre, Copenhagen.
– *En Sælgers Liv* (*A Salesman's Life*) on Percy von Halling-Koch, presented by Hans-Georg Møller, broadcast nationally in Denmark, 27 February 1980 (National Library of Sweden, KB, Audiovisual Archive, Stockholm).

Interviews

Anders Byriel, 21 March 2012, Kvadrat HQ, Ebeltoft, Denmark.
Poul Byriel, 22 March 2012, Kvadrat HQ, Ebeltoft, Denmark.
Erling Rasmussen, 22 March 2012, Kvadrat HQ, Ebeltoft, Denmark.
Anne Jørgensen, 21 March 2012, Kvadrat HQ, Ebeltoft, Denmark.
David Nelson, by telephone, 5 July 2012.

Alfredo Häberli, *Village*, 2008
Åsa Pärson, *Molly*, 2004
Finn Sködt, *Divina 3*, 2007
Anne Fabricius Møller and Bodil Jerichau, *Onyx*, 2010
Finn Sködt, *Divina MD*, 2012
Tord Boontje, *Shadow*, 2005
Åsa Pärson, *Missing Thread*, 2007
Frans Dijkmeijer, *Colline*, 2012
Ole Kortzau, *Waves*, 1978
Helene Vonsild, *Chicago*, 2006
Alfredo Häberli, *Highfield*, 2008
Guilio Ridolfo and Frans Dijkmeijer, *Steelcut Trio*, 2006
Aggebo & Henriksen, *Felicia*, 2000
Satu Montanari, *Pause*, 1993
Frans Dijkmeijer, *Vale*, 2012
Finn Sködt, *Divina Melange*, 1999
Tord Boontje, *Nectar*, 2005
Nina Koppel, *Tonus*, 1974
Erik Ole Jørgensen, *Time*, 1987
Patricia Urquiola, *Winding*, 2013
Georgina Wright, *Tonica*, 2000
Akira Minagawa, *Hallingdal Tambourine*, 2006
Giulio Ridolfo, Remix 2, 2012
Frans Dijkmeijer, *Ripple*, 2012
Karina Nielsen Rios, *Checkpoint*, 2008
Nanna Ditzel, *Hallingdal*, 1965

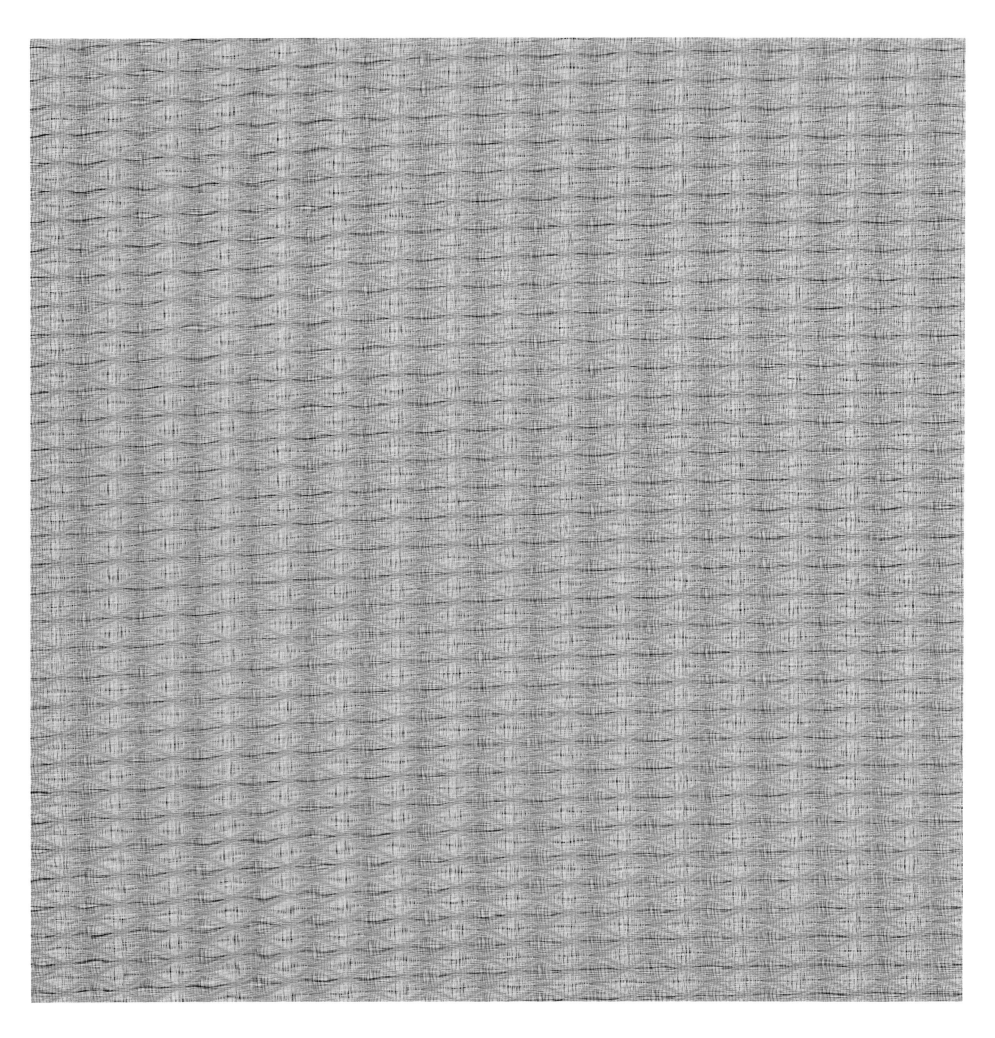

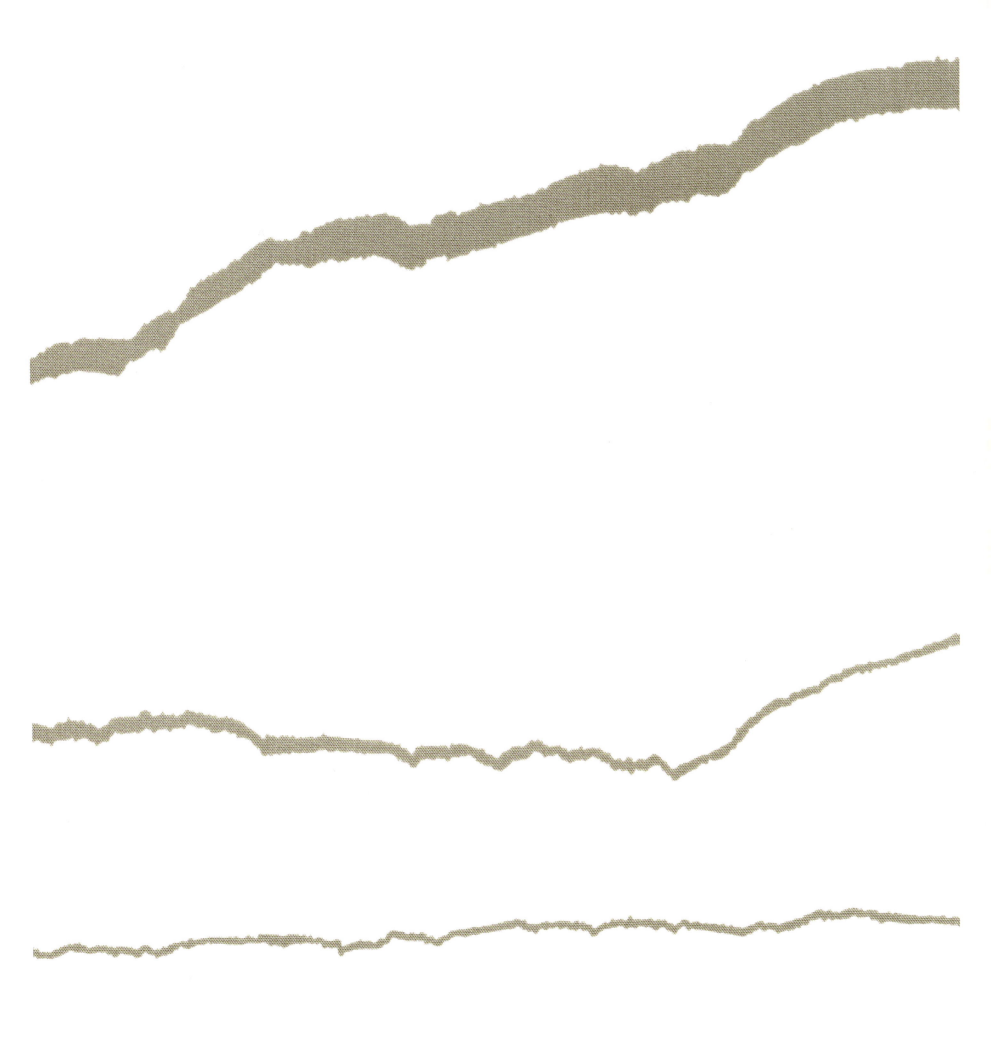

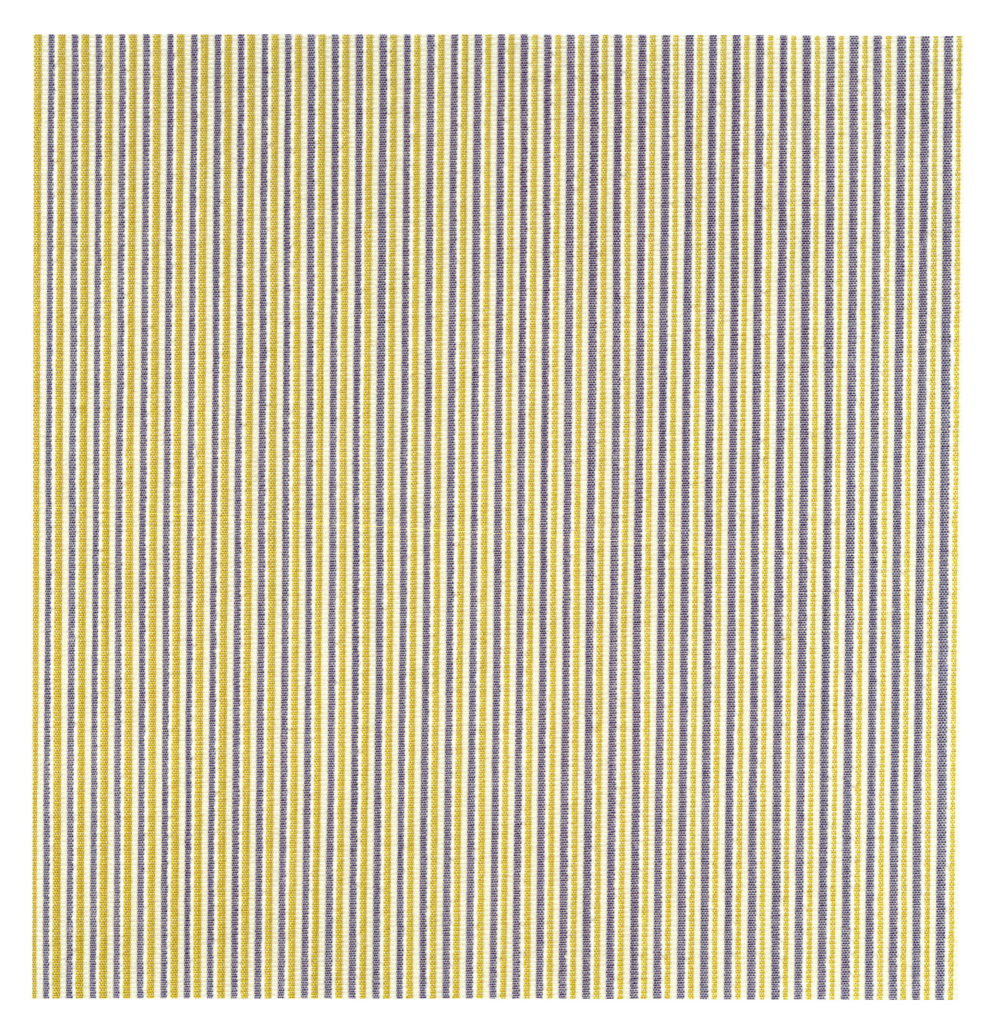

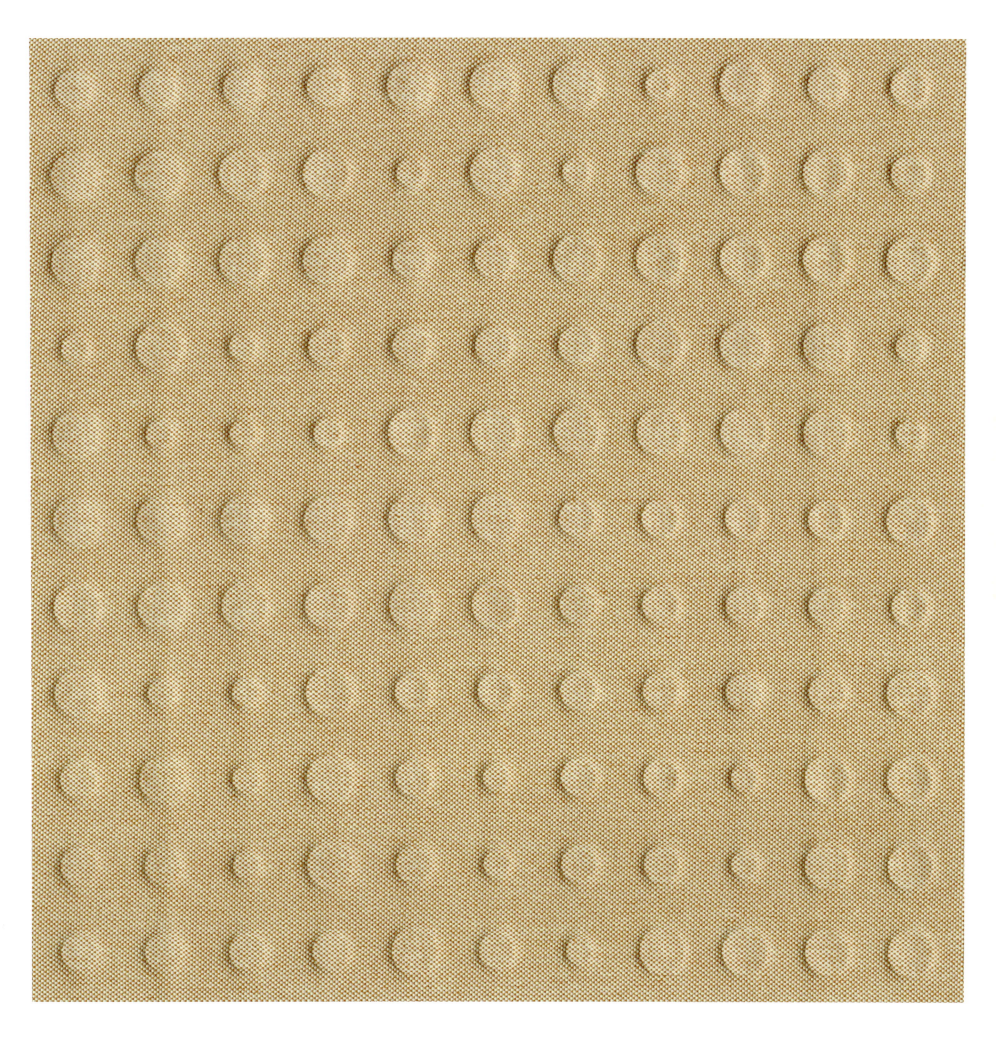

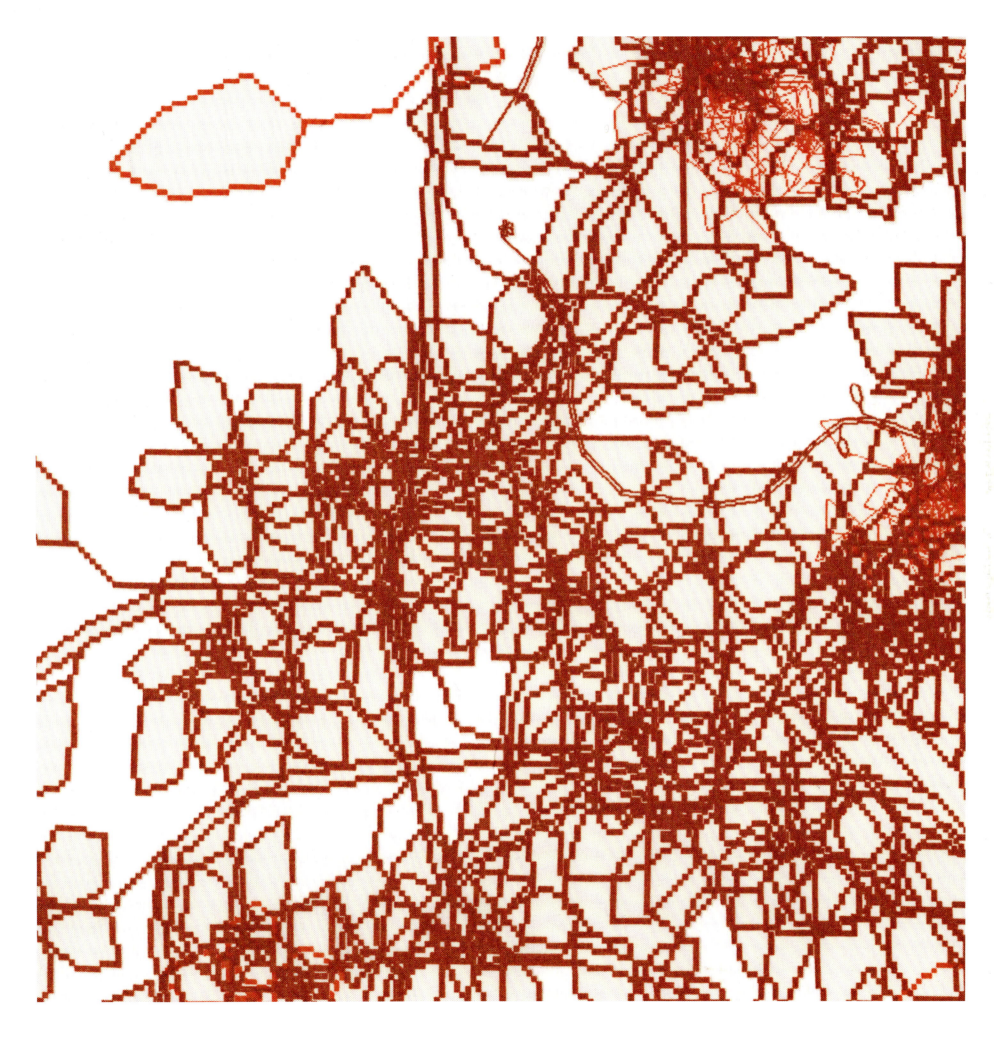

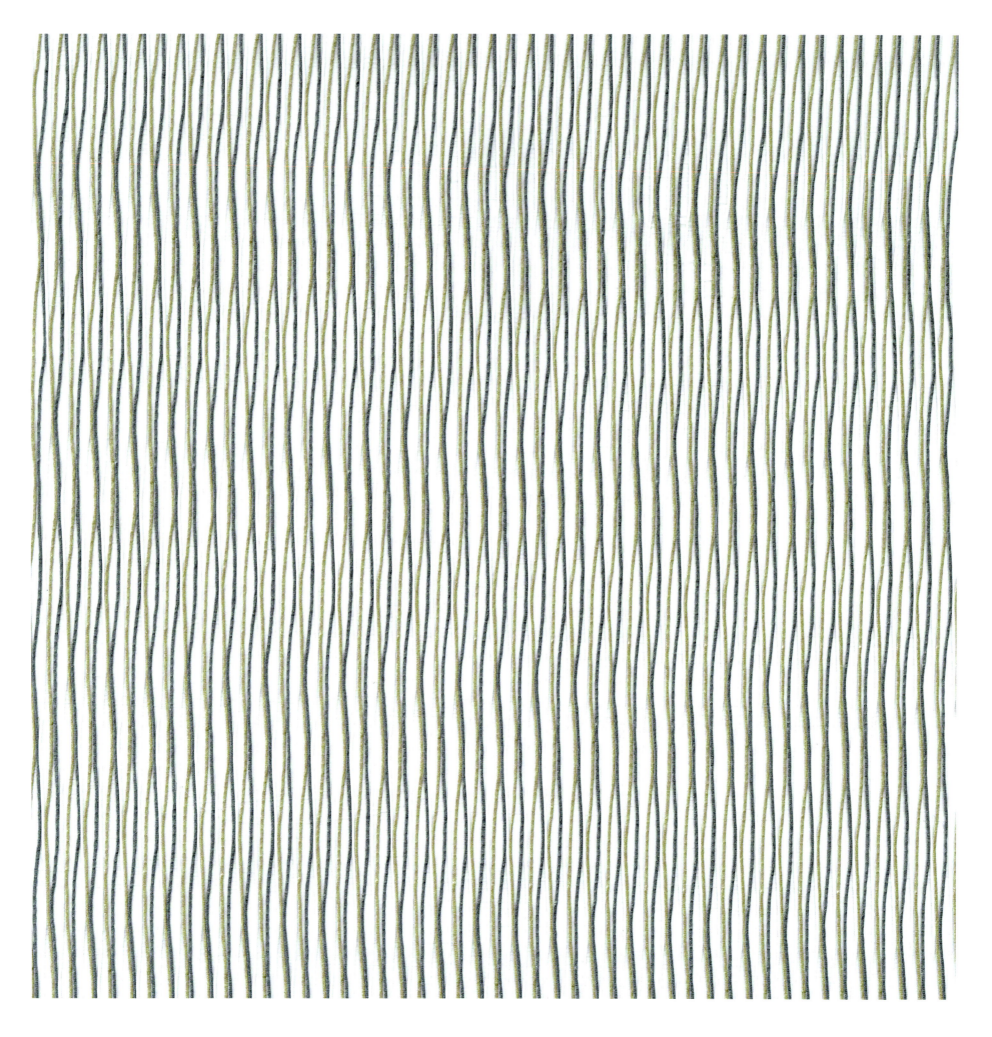

Jane Withers

Between artifice and nature:
colour since the 1960s

'One sits more comfortably on a colour that one likes.'
 Verner Panton

'Colour is stronger than language. It's a subliminal
 communication.' Louise Bourgeois

In 1909, Henry Ford made his famous declaration of standardisation: 'Any customer can have a car painted any colour that he wants so long as it is black.' Almost exactly a century later, Apple was challenged in court over its use of the slogan 'Millions of Colors' to promote its computer equivalent of the *Model T*. These two examples illustrate – almost too neatly – how from the late nineteenth century to today there has been an almost unimaginable shift in the availability and possibilities of colour, colour technologies and our experience and expectations of colour, all of which have snowballed exponentially, from the limited and gradually changing palette of the pre-Victorian era and the first chemically manufactured paints, via the invention of scientific colour systems such as the Pantone chart, to the potential for a seemingly infinite virtual palette of digital colours projected magically on our computer screens and phones for our use and play.

The Danish textile company Kvadrat emerged almost exactly at the mid point in what might be described as the century of colour, and has since played a significant role in colouring furniture and modern interiors. In the history of the evolution of colour and design in the last half century, a handful of episodes and collaborations stand out as particularly significant in shaping the interior landscape of colour and its influence on the design world. And Kvadrat's role in the story is pivotal.

While modern industry has tended to promote colour in terms of quantity and choice and has given us hugely expanded palettes that can be accurately reproduced at relatively low cost, that is only part of the story. Arguably, artists' and designers' more experimental approach to colour and their pioneering interpretations of new colour technologies have been equally – if not more – influential in shaping colour aesthetics and how we use and relate to colour.

From the outset, Kvadrat operated in a progressive design world and responded to directions set by the designers, architects and artists around it. It is this experimental cultural milieu and a series of significant collaborations that have been instrumental in pushing the boundaries of colour and textiles in interiors and in propelling Kvadrat to the centre of design developments.

The palette of pop

In a world already thrown open to change, 1968 was a cataclysmic year across Europe – from explosive politics and student revolutions to pop art and its brilliant candy-colours that reflected the new social order. It was also the year that Kvadrat was founded in the small town of Ebeltoft on the Danish coast. Scandinavia was a good place to be at the time, as the influence of visionary Nordic designers – Eero Saarinen, Arne Jacobsen, Verner Panton, Gunnar Aagaard Andersen, Nanna Ditzel, Eero Aarnio and Marimekko among others – reverberated way beyond that region's borders. From the outset, it could be argued that Kvadrat's unofficial mission was to provide the palette to colour this brave new futuristic organic interior landscape and the pop aesthetic that was in the process of emerging.

As much as anything else, what pop revolutionised was colour. In contrast to the traditional artists' painterly palette, rooted in the natural world and its flora and fauna, pop treated colour as ready-made, and borrowed bold hues from the garage forecourt, supermarket shelves, commercial paint charts and the mass media. Roland Barthes's observation that the colour of pop was 'chemical' referred to the bold contrast of saturated primaries as well as the fact that it no longer made use of oil paints or artists' colours but borrowed colour directly from industry. The artificial flavourings of Warhol's many *Marilyns* came from commercial screen-printing inks applied on canvas; Frank Stella used a standard range of alkyd wall paints – a form of polyester with an even matt surface – manufactured by the Brooklyn paint company Benjamin Moore; Donald

Frank Stella, *Single Concentric Squares (violet to red violet half-step)*, 1974

Above: Verner Panton, *Restaurant Varna*, 1971 (Aarhus, Denmark)
Facing Page: Verner Panton, *Astoria Retaurant*, 1960 (Trondheim, Norway)

Judd – following Richard Hamilton and John Chamberlain – adopted high-gloss lacquers such as motorcycle paints (Harley Davidson's Hi-Fi red and Hi-Fi purple). The chemical effect turned colour from the natural, with all nature's variegations, into a single smooth industrially manufactured entity, a lipstick-like surface appeal, celebrated in the mesmerising title of Tom Wolfe's book *The Kandy-Kolored Tangerine-Flake Streamline Baby*. As artist and writer David Batchelor notes in *Chromophobia*, 'The colours of the modern city are almost all entirely new and completely unnatural. Most of the colours we now see are chemical or electrical; they are plastic or metallic; they are flat, shiny, glowing or flashing.'

This brave new colour explosion came right up to Kvadrat's doorstep: Verner Panton and Nanna Ditzel were key figures in overthrowing the colourlessness of the muted, wood-toned monochromes of Danish design in the 1950s and early 1960s and translating pop's abstract and graphic approach to colour through to the material world. Although Panton worked with other textile companies – first the Danish Unika Væv and then the Swiss company Mira-X – his world was closely connected to Kvadrat. Kvadrat's founders Poul Byriel and Erling Rasmussen worked together at Unika Væv under the directorship of the flamboyant Percy von

Halling-Koch (known affectionately as 'Bum'), at a time when the pioneering textile company was championing the new Danish design being disseminated via Gunnar Bratvold's influential design magazine *Mobilia*.

Panton has been described as a 'creator of atmospheres for living spaces', and essentially these atmospheres were founded on colour. 'One sits more comfortably on a colour that one likes', Panton wrote in *Notes on Colour*, the book which collected his personal comments on the perception of colour alongside his reflections on both ancient and modern colour theories as well as the more technical colour systems employed by modern industry.

Panton followed Goethe and Kandinsky in their belief in the psychic and spiritual meaning of colours and their psychological and sensual effect on the environment and hence people. 'Colour planning is of utmost importance when creating a milieu. It is not enough to say that red is red and blue is blue. I myself normally work with parallel colours whose tones follow consecutively according to the order of the spectrum. In this way, I can control the character of the room in terms of warmth and coolness and thereby create the desired atmosphere.' Working with the six prismatic colours – the three primary colours and three secondary colours – he distinguished between

warm and cool palettes to create moods that corresponded to the purpose of a room: 'Green for example is given priority in rooms in which a calm atmosphere is required'. He frequently used interior landscapes of greens and blues in schemes for offices, whereas the clubs and restaurants he designed pulsate in over-heated, retina-warping contrasts of purple, red and orange.

Colour as a psychological and sensual element reached full expression in Panton's trippy spatial installations, which wove together architecture, furniture and light to create total coloured environments such as the *Astoria* (1960) in Trondheim, Norway, and *Restaurant Varna* (1971) in Aarhus, where Panton allowed the floor, ceiling and walls, furniture, lamps, mirrors and textiles to merge, melt and blend into one single close-knit entity where individual objects seem almost to 'grow' out of the room. Colour gives definition to this open spatial flow, using pulsating hues to create an unreal, mood-altering ambience. In *Notes on Colour* he wrote, 'There is an incredible number of people who fight against the use of colours. But there are also many people who fight against common sense.'

The most influential fabric in terms of bringing colour to this bold new graphic-design language was undoubtedly Nanna Ditzel's *Hallingdal*, designed originally for the Halling-Koch Design Center in 1965 and

Verner Panton, colour plan for *Restaurant Varna*, 1971 (Aarhus, Denmark)

Verner Panton, *Restaurant Varna*, 1971 (Aarhus, Denmark)

Nanna Ditzel, *Stairscape*, 1966 (created for Unika Væv showroom)
Facing page: Nanna Ditzel, *Hallingdal*, 1965

associated from the start with such revolutionary designs as Arne Jacobsen's *Egg* and *Swan* chairs. Within a few years the marketing was taken over by Kvadrat, and the textile has been the company's bestseller ever since. From the beginning *Hallingdal* was available in 42 colours, and it is revealing that the colour range is not based on an industrial colour system but on Ditzel's own highly refined and idiosyncratic colour sense. While still using bright colours, she moved from pop's primaries to a more harmonious palette that has been described as bright pastels. The range eventually grew from 42 to 105 colours and was updated by Ditzel every five to ten years until her death in 2005. In the 2012 update, part of her original harmonic colour scheme was restored. Among the constants have been Ditzel's favourite colours – a hot pink and a vivid turquoise. Photos of Ditzel's house in 1966 show platform seating in soft lipstick pink and reds set off against a mauve blue. Ditzel's striking sense of colour infiltrated the Kvadrat universe in other ways: she coloured the interior of their second office, the schoolhouse, painting the balustrade in a luminous palette of blues and pinks.

Hallingdal and the collaboration with Ditzel established a working pattern that Kvadrat has followed ever since, by inviting artists or designers to develop colour ranges for a specific fabric – ranges that are deliberately large enough to provide architects and designers with a diverse palette but that are also governed by a strong individual aesthetic. In the early 1980s Kvadrat began a long collaboration with poetic colourist Finn Sködt, best known for the textile *Divina*. Sködt first worked for the company as a graphic designer, but his influence soon extended to textile colour and also to the way fabrics were presented in sample books and in the company's showrooms. Sködt sees textiles as a means of bringing softness and colour into the interior, and works from an instinctive understanding of colour and its effect on material that's informed by memory, recognition and the emotional effects of colour rather than fashion or scientifically formulated systems. According to Sködt, 'Colours have an autonomy about them, an ability to elude any system. They should be perceived in the pigment and in the fabric and not in any system.'

Divina's success – like *Hallingdal*'s – can be attributed largely to its extraordinary colour range, which is periodically refreshed by Sködt. One of the boldest recent uses of *Divina* is artist Liam Gillick's seating installation *Prototype Conference Room* for the auditorium at the Whitechapel Gallery, London, where contrasting colours hum and zing, sweetie-wrapper pink riffing against canary yellow, Belisha orange against Yves Klein blue. The effect is a strange, even slightly uneasy, hybrid of institutional and groovy; a bit Bauhaus, a bit Donald Judd; a bit psychedelic; strikingly unfamiliar.

And Kvadrat's colour evolution is ongoing. An important current collaboration is with the Italian fashion textile and colour adviser Giulio Ridolfo. Ridolfo brings a fashion sensibility to furnishing textiles, and what he describes as an 'Italian eye' to balance the cooler aesthetic associated with the watery Scandinavian light and landscape and Modernist terrain from which Kvadrat sprang. Ridolfo's first collaborations in the furniture industry were with Italian manufacturer Moroso and designer Patricia Urquiola. Here he was instrumental in shaping a material patchwork of pattern and colour characterised by 'off' colours and a delicacy and vivaciousness – even femininity – that are very different from the graphic boldness and saturated colours generally associated with Modernist design. Ridolfo describes fabric as the 'robe' that dresses furniture; 'the surface that has to appeal both visually and tactilely as well as looking good under any lighting conditions'. He experiments with materials, patterns and colours until the product is 'dressed' correctly and he has given it an identity. For Urquiola's urbane *Fjord chair*, for example, the

Nanna Ditzel, Kvadrat showroom, 1970 (Ebeltoft)

Below: Finn Sködt, *Divina* colour palette from 1989
Facing page: Liam Gillick, *Prototype Conference Room*, 2009 (Zilkha Auditorium of the Whitechapel Gallery, London)

Above: detail of Feuilles de Choux tapestry panel (Flemish, 16th century, Langeais Castle, France)
Facing page: Ronan & Erwan Bouroullec, *North Tiles*, 2009 (Kvadrat's Stockholm showroom)

Above and facing page: Patricia Urquiola and Giulio Ridolfo, *The Dwelling Lab*, 2010,
(in collaboration with BMW, Kvadrat showroom, Milan)

prominent seams give it a tailored appearance
that's softened by the subtle play of surface pattern
and colour.

Ridolfo's starting point is the character of the fabric
that is to be coloured – whether cotton, wool or plastic
– and its weave. His first colour scale for a Kvadrat fabric
was for *Steelcut* (designed by the Dutch weaving master
Frans Dijkmeijer), a strong weave to which Ridolfo's
colouring brings a more organic feel. *Steelcut Trio* is
composed of three different colours which he describes
as 'complex mixes with something missing, something
irregular, an imperfection that permits a different
kind of harmony.' Ridolfo builds these purposefully
idiosyncratic and skewed colour palettes by assem-
bling objects to create families of colours and textures.
But while composing the colour palette might, on the
surface, seem like the colourist's main task, in reality
this is only the beginning. Each new colour then takes
six to eight months to evolve from proposal to final
fabric range, in a process that involves mixing a dye
formula that can be guaranteed to produce the same
results time after time.

Like Panton, Ridolfo sees a psychological dimension
in the way textiles and colour interact in an interior,
conditioning mood and influencing social interaction. 'How will we read a textile? Is it destined for the

beach or the seventh floor of a skyscraper? What do
people need? There's no longer a need to surprise in a
public space. Instead we need to create a setting where
people can interact. In a restaurant we need to make
people feel comfortable, make them talk and feel good
together. It is more about inner values and textiles
can help create the setting for this.'

In collaboration with BMW, Kvadrat invited Ridolfo
and Urquiola to revisit the car interior. 'They asked us
to reconsider the big bourgeois car, the *Gran Turismo*,
and of course executive tastes. Leather, beige, shiny
wood: it is the same for all executive cars and planes,
but I don't believe anyone really likes it. What is needed
is to reconsider the boundaries of luxe and good taste.'
Ridolfo and Urquiola produced a tactile padded textile
interior in a warm beige spiked with fluorescent
flashes. According to Ridolfo, 'It was about a provo-
cation – it used *Remix* and *Divina* to tone down the car
interior. There is always a lot of visual pollution in the
car. You are seated for a long time but you don't enjoy
your sofa.' Although this project has yet to have much
perceptible influence on car interiors, it is underpinned
by an imaginative approach to colour and textiles
that has the potential to make industrial objects more
nuanced and subtly meaningful.

Virtual colour

From the birth of egg tempera to the invention of
synthetic paints, new technologies have influenced
and even transformed artists' and designers' approaches
to colour, and without doubt the biggest step since
pop's celebration of chemical colour is the emergence
of digital colour. Instead of natural plant roots, leaves
and petals, or laboratory test tubes, virtual colour is
brought to us in immaterial byte-sized pixels and every
computer, tablet or phone offers a practically infinite
menu of ready-made colours. The glowing screen has
created an aesthetic even more alluring and evanescent
than the glossy world of pop; a virtualisation of colour
that paradoxically appears both intangible and more
mesmerizingly hyper-real than anything the analogue
colours of the material world can match. In *Chromophobia*,
David Batchelor draws a distinction between analogical
and digital colour. 'The colour circle', he writes, 'is
analogical; the colour chart is digital. Analogical colour
is a continuum, a seamless spectrum, an undivided
whole, a merging of one colour into another. Digital
colour is individuated; it comes in discrete units;
there is not mergence or modulation; there are only
boundaries, steps and edges. Analogical colour is colour;
digital colour is colours.'

Below: Aggebo and Henriksen, *Waterborn*, 2010
Facing page: Aggebo and Henriksen, details of urban snapshots used as a colour source for *Waterborn*

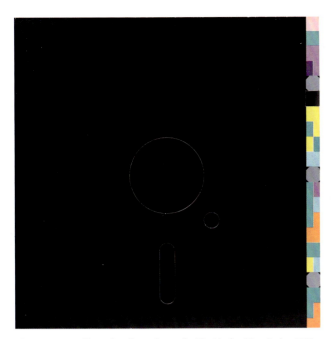

Above: Peter Saville Studio, sleeve design for *Blue Monday*, New Order, 1983
Facing page: David Adjaye and Peter Saville, Kvadrat showroom, London, 2009

The immersive allure of colour is both subject and object of the collaboration between art director Peter Saville and architect David Adjaye in Kvadrat's London showroom. The Victorian warehouse has been hollowed out and coated in matt black to act as a vacuum-like foil to the dominant element: a stairway lined with a spectrum-coloured glass balustrade. Emphasizing the synergy between a place and its purpose, this rainbow bath of coloured light is an obvious reference to the importance of colour to Kvadrat, but also to Saville's 1983 design for the record sleeve for New Order's *Blue Monday*, which famously did not print the title or the band's name, but used blocks of colour as a code with which to transmit them, rather like a coloured barcode.

We have seen from the beginning how Kvadrat has responded to the artists and designers circling around the company and looked to them for influence and the impetus for new directions. In the last decade CEO Anders Byriel has been instrumental (as his father Poul Byriel and Erling Rasmussen were before him) in gathering a network of collaborators whose work does not necessarily relate directly to textile design, but whose influence becomes apparent from time to time. At the entrance to the company's Ebeltoft headquarters is a chandelier by Olafur Eliasson, a relative

of his immense kaleidoscopic chandeliers hanging in Copenhagen's opera house. Last summer Günther Vogt and Eliasson completed the landscape work *Your glacial expectations*, surrounding Kvadrat's offices. It will be interesting to see how this collaboration evolves, although early attempts to translate Eliasson's aesthetic to textiles have proved challenging for contemporary colour technologies.

While op art and pop art rejected nature as the root of colour in favour of a chemically induced palette, Eliasson's work returns to nature, but nature as refracted through technology; it is an investigation into our perception of light and colour. Natural phenomena form a basis for his art, but they're catapulted into an extra-terrestrial dimension. In Tate Modern's Turbine Hall, his *Weather project* becomes a sunset beyond natural human experience. In Aarhus, the installation *Your rainbow panorama* immerses visitors in the colours of the rainbow but with the brightness dial turned to max. While these works dematerialise colour, they also make it the medium of existence. Colour is no longer fixed, but fleeting and evanescent, like the effect of light on the dichromatic and reflective glass surfaces of Eliasson and Henning Larsen Architects' façade for the *Harpa Reykjavik Concert Hall and Conference Centre*. If colour is a continuously evolving

narrative, in parallel with developments in other fields like genetics or environmental science, there is a sense that it has entered a new discourse between nature and artifice, analogue and digital, virtual and material, where these are no longer segregated or in opposition, but breeding new hybrids, engaged in a constantly evolving relationship.

Above and facing page: Olafur Eliasson, *Your rainbow panorama*, 2011 (Aarhus, Denmark)

In celebration of *Hallingdal*, Kvadrat invited a new generation of designers to create works using the textile, exploring new applications for the fabric.

The commissioned pieces were curated by Tord Boontje, Ilse Crawford, Søren Rose, Constance Rubini, Hans Maier-Aichen, Jeffrey Bernett and Andre Fu, with executive curators Patrizia Moroso and Giulio Ridolfo, and exhibited as *Hallingdal 65* at the Salone Internazionale del Mobile, Milan, 2012.

Jean-Baptiste Fastrez, *Quetzacoalt*
Emphasising the volume of a traditional hammock shape, Jean-Baptiste Fastrez used fabric tubes of different sizes that he then cut and tied on to a net, creating a thick 'fur'. *Quetzacoalt* was inspired both by traditional African costumes and techniques used for military camouflage.

Raw-Edges Design Studio, *Selvedge*
Unravelling and releasing threads from within the woven fabric to create a hollow sleeve within it, Raw-Edges then placed two layers of *Hallingdal* in different colours on top of one another, creating a colourful rim, reminiscent of the selvedge that hems raw fabrics. By deconstructing the fabric, they emphasised the beauty of its structural qualities.

Front, *Hallingdal Fringe*
Using cut-offs of *Hallingdal* produced as by-products of the furniture production process, the design group Front created a patchwork quilt. When washed, and with ongoing use, the raw hems dissolve, leaving a fringed effect that gives the whole a three-dimensional character.

Hjortefar, *Bum and Nanna*
Inspired by stories of 'Bum' – the exuberant Baron Percy von Halling-Koch, the entrepreneur whose name *Hallingdal* bears – Hjortefar made him the subject of a double portrait together with the designer Nanna Ditzel. Created using 5cm × 5cm 'pixels' (small padded pieces backed with MDF) the portraits were made in part by inmates of the Vridsløselille State Prison.

Ionna Vautrin, *Zoo*
A series of bright, colourful, oversized pillows in the shapes of a toucan, panda bear and whale, each animal in Ionna Vautrin's *Zoo* is around the same proportions as a small child, making them particularly huggable. The zoo can be added to over time with the addition of new species.

Fredrikson Stallard, *Halligdal Table*
Like wood, *Hallingdal* fabric is constructed from fibres – packed sufficiently tightly it will become, like wood, a strong and solid material. In a play on multiple contrasts, Fredrikson Stallard's *Hallingdal Table* binds a tightly wound roll of fabric – reminiscent of a sliced tree trunk – using an industrial ratchet strap with a gold-plated buckle.

BLESS, Nº35 *Automatica Carcanapé*
Using their skills in fashion as well as design, BLESS offer a tongue-in-cheek bespoke car cover service for supercars. Impeccably fitted to the contours of your four-wheeled status symbol, the cover can also be stuffed with foam and used as a piece of furniture.

Mermeladaestudio, *Welcome*
An indoor playhouse for children, the form of *Welcome* – part rocket, part tipi, part igloo – lends itself to imaginative play. Supported by five feet, *Welcome* has a padded base and a skeletal structure of rings covered in two different colours of *Hallingdal* and is embroidered on the inside with geometric graphics.

Hettie Judah

Tord Boontje: ornamentation
and a new aesthetic

Tord Boontje, *Happy Ever After*, 2004 (installation for Moroso, Milan)

'Broadly speaking, one may say that the use of this subordinate, but by no means unimportant art is to enliven with beauty and incident what would otherwise be a blank space, wheresoever or whatsoever it may be.'
—William Morris, *The History of Pattern Designing*, 1879

Tord Boontje is a great enlivener of blank space. He makes light dance, ducking and twisting through shadows of tangled wire flora and silhouettes of forest creatures, springing refracted off crystals and sidling through cut cloth. Mythical beasts trip off his tableware and squirrels peep out from his shoe patterns. In his hands, the everyday and overlooked develop potent life; cherry pips become jewels, shattered glass the basis for a textile pattern, and wildflowers a print-making tool for ceramics.

In April 2004, he created a magical, all-enveloping installation for the Italian manufacturers Moroso. *Happy Ever After* was designed at the invitation of Patrizia Moroso, and acted as the brand's showpiece for that year's Milan furniture fair. Flickering, colourful, jangly and kinetic, the installation was, even by Boontje's own admission, over the top, but it was joyously so, and in its use of decorative handmade elements such as embroidery, it brought a human

edge to the too often bland and featureless world of the Milan fair.

A longtime collaborator with that master showman of the fashion world, Alexander McQueen, Boontje created chair 'characters' to people his installation for Moroso, dressing them as though for a fairytale catwalk – a witch chair in black leather, a pirate swagged with cord and embroidery and, like the bride at the end of the show, a princess chair in tulle skirts. Using woollen textiles supplied by the sponsor Kvadrat, heavy laser-cut garlands hung from fabric vines and fine floral-printed voile shivered in the breeze between painted walls and crystal-iced branches.

'Tord's show at that fair was a total new world,' recalls Anne Jørgensen, Kvadrat's design director. 'It was very inspiring for all of us.' Once the Milan fair was over, Anne and CEO Anders Byriel went to visit Tord at his studio in London to discuss the possibility of a new working relationship that would bring his tangled, romantic vision into the then more aesthetically reserved world of Kvadrat.

'Now if you should think I have got on to matters over serious for our small subject of pattern-designing, I will say, first, that even these lesser arts, being produced by man's intelligence, cannot really

be separated from the greater, the more purely intellectual ones, or from the life which creates both.'
—William Morris, *The History of Pattern Designing*, 1879

Born in the Netherlands in 1968 to a Swedish mother and Dutch father, Boontje had a creative, outdoorsy upbringing, and was interested in design from an early age. His studies at the famously challenging and iconoclastic Design Academy Eindhoven were followed by a postgraduate course at the Royal College of Art in London, where he is now head of the Design Products department.

The projects that first brought Boontje to the attention of the design world in the 1990s were far from the lush decorative aesthetic for which he is best known today. The *tranSglass* (1997–present) and *Rough and Ready* (1998) collections both worked with humble materials and a visual language that emerged from a ruthless honesty about their origins and manufacture. A set of containers made from used glass bottles, *tranSglass* was a project conceived in collaboration with Boontje's wife, the glass artist Emma Woffenden, and eventually became part of his portfolio of ethical manufacturing projects produced under Artecnica's Design w/Conscience label. *Rough and Ready* was a range of ultra-simple make-it-yourself furniture designs

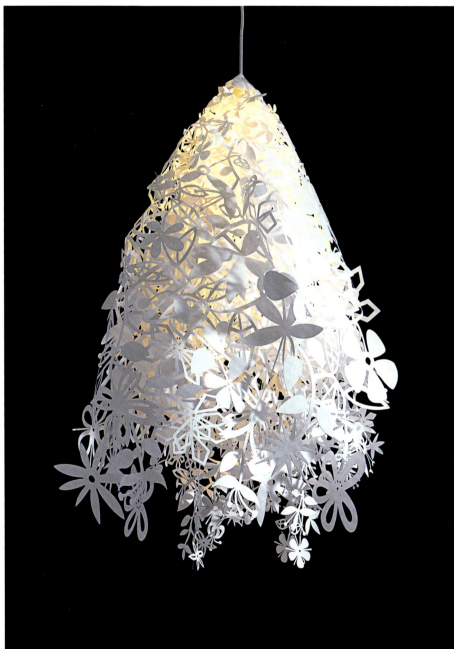

Above: Tord Boontje, *Garland light*, 2002 (produced by Habitat and Artecnica)
Facing page: Tord Boontje, *Midsummer light*, 2005 (produced for *Carousel* installation,
Alexander McQueen store, Milan)

Tord Boontje, *Midsummer light*, 2004 (produced by Artecnica)

Above: Tord Boontje and Emma Woffenden, *tranSglass*, 1997 (produced by Artecnica since 2005)
Opposite: Tord Boontje, *Rough and Ready*, 1998

which anyone could construct from recycled or cheap materials such as 2cm × 2cm softwood strips, plywood and army blankets.

A more familiar dark, pastoral lyricism came into Boontje's work with *Wednesday* (2001), a collection commissioned by the British Council for exhibition in Prague. The collection included ingenious blown-glass pieces patterned by the impress of nails hammered into a board, a perforated metal-topped table and a floral lampshade etched out of thin sheet metal that would, as the *Garland light* for Habitat, go on to become Boontje's first hit mass-market product and a startling decorative intrusion into the determinedly pared-back design market.

Commissions from Swarovski followed, as did a number of new products for Artecnica, including the internationally successful *Midsummer Light*, which was launched in January 2004, shortly before Boontje was approached by Patrizia Moroso to create the installation that made him famous and catalysed his working relationship with Kvadrat.

'Is it not better to be reminded, however simply, of the close vine-trellis that keeps out the sun by the Nile side; or of the wild-woods and their streams, with the dogs panting beside them;

or of the swallows sweeping above the garden boughs toward the house-eaves where their nestlings are, while the sun breaks [through] the clouds on them; or of the many-flowered summer meadows of Picardy?'
– William Morris, *Some Hints on Pattern Designing*, 1881

While *Happy Ever After* contained a number of experimental fabrics, including laser cuts, digital prints and computer-generated pattern, Boontje had not at that stage worked commercially in textiles. It was, however, a discipline with which he had strong and resonant ties – his grandmother was a weaver and his mother a textile designer and costume historian. Knitting, embroidery and weaving were all part of the creative milieu of hand-working in which he had grown up.

The background that Boontje brought into his first collection of designs for Kvadrat in 2005 was not only technical but cultural. Expanding on the revitalised, modern florals that had cascaded over the installation at Moroso, he presented a portfolio straight out of the wild woods of the North, dappled with their forest sunlight and stained with their folklore. It included a pair of briar-rose designs, *Prince* and *Princess*, that when printed over one another created a new pattern

called *Happy*, and a hand-drawn fantasy garden called *Wilderness*, complete with peeping wildlife so furtive-looking that one imagined it might speak.

The natural aspect of the collection was offset by a sharply artificial colour palette, using a set of ramped up, feverish tones that nodded to the works of rococo artist François Boucher. 'I start with the pattern and then the colour comes later,' he explains. 'For the first collection it was like a mechanism – once you see what the selection of patterns is going to be, all very floral and natural, then maybe it's good to counterbalance that too, make it not all natural and not too healthy, a bit synthetic as well.'

The colours were inspired by paintings from the Wallace Collection in London. Boontje has something like perfect pitch for colour, and reproduced elements from the palette of the Boucher paintings when he returned to his studio. While studying at Eindhoven, Boontje had started to build up a box of original colours – he worked regularly in paint, and when he created a tone that pleased him he'd paint the wash on to a separate piece of paper and save it in the box for future projects. He also reproduced colours that inspired him from works of art and nature, building up a portfolio of subtle but

Tord Boontje, *Princess*, 2005

Above: Tord Boontje, *Prince*, 2005
Facing page: Tord Boontje, *Happy*, 2005

Right: Tord Boontje, artwork for *Wilderness*, 2005
Facing page: *Wilderness*, 2005 (final fabric)

Above: François Boucher, *An Autumn Pastoral*, 1749
Facing page: Tord Boontje, *Magic*, 2005

François Boucher, *Madame de Pompadour*, 1759

original tones. It is, as he says, 'much better than having a Pantone book'.

Cuttings of Boontje's Boucher-inspired colour record cards were sent to Kvadrat, who matched the tones both for plain and printed fabrics. The company also developed a new lightweight woollen cloth, appropriately called *Magic*, which was easier to print on to than their classic *Divina*. 'The first collection with him was very bright in colours,' recalls Anne Jørgensen. 'It was very fresh coming in with these flowers – the techniques, designs and bright colours were all quite new for us. People remember the Tord collection – if you have seen a sofa or chair with those big flowers on, you remember it forever.'

Rather than taking a modest toe-dip into the floral world, Kvadrat opted to launch an extensive range of pattern, only available in Boontje's own colours. Manufacturing the collection was a wide-ranging and international process. 'The printers are in Germany and Switzerland; the wool is woven in Scotland. The burn-out is done in Japan; the laser cutting in Italy,' he recalls. 'But it was quite straightforward.' Everything returned to the company's headquarters in Ebeltoft for the final selection; vast samples were rolled out all over the office building. It was an ornamental takeover.

'Every material in which household goods are fashioned imposes certain special limitations within which the craftsman must work […] these limitations are as far as possible from being hindrances to beauty in the several crafts. On the contrary, they are incitements and helps to its attainment.'
–William Morris, *Some Hints on Pattern Designing*, 1881

Boontje created a second collection for Kvadrat in 2009, this time moving away from the floral theme, which he felt had become too popular and recognizable, and towards more abstract patterns. Preparatory artwork for this included experiments with ink bleeding into damp paper, and an intense mesh of scribbled lines in coloured pen, both of which led to rather unexpected fabric patterns. Together with his wife Emma Woffenden, he created the *Anima Animus* exhibition for the Glass Museum in Ebeltoft, which contextualised many of his fabric designs, including the streaked red curtain fabric designed for Kvadrat and placed around an earlier chair, dripping visceral red resin. It also led to the commission of a design that resembled broken glass: one of Boontje's fetish objects in his appreciation of everyday beauty. 'I really like shattered panes of glass. I'd always had the idea to make curtains that when you

closed them looked like someone had smashed the glass,' he says. 'They look like diamonds.'

As with the first collection, Boontje thought not only about creating new designs, but also about expanding the way that pattern was used and how it behaved. For the first collection he had hand-drawn the briar-rose patterns, then scanned them in low resolution to make the lines of the pattern fragile and broken up. For the new collection, the thick mesh of scribbled lines was scanned, then blown up until each line was thicker than a finger, and the incidental webbing and graduations in intensity created a pattern of their own. The design was then jacquard-woven and boiled to create a woollen felted cloth called *Elements* that, like the fragile lines of the rose pattern, felt worn- in and soft at the edges.

The random quality of the hand-drawn lines translated in the cloth into the shifting suggestion of patterns from nature – in grey, it became speckled stone; in blue, ripples of water; in green, stippled moss. The imperfection in *Elements* is what makes the design so easy to incorporate into an existing space – it is an industrially produced product that nevertheless shows evidence of the designer's hand.

This combination of hand and machine manufacture defines a key element in the relationship between

Wool Quality 1st priority

W1 Red

W2 lemon

W3 lime

W4 terra cotta

W5 magenta

W6 water green

W7 dark green

W8 cream

W9 dark purple

W10 light blue

W11 blue

W12 pink lilac

Wool Quality 2nd priority

W13 Rasberry

W14 purple

W15 pale orange

W16 Indigo

W17 light grey

W18 dark grey

W19 green

W20 pink orange

Above: Tord Boontje's hand-painted colour cards for his 2005 collection with Kvadrat
Facing page: Tord Boontje's colour studies for *Tarentel*, 2009

Wool Threads Print

Background

V1   V2

V1   V2

Tord Boontje, drawing experiment in coloured pen that led to *Elements*, 2009

Tord Boontje, drawing experiment with ink and damp paper that led to *Tarentel*, 2009

Above: Alfred Hitchcock, still from *Rebecca*, 1940
Facing page: Tord Boontje, *Shadow*, 2005

Boontje and Kvadrat; one that the designer character-ises as being artisan in aesthetic and industrial in production. So long as a design could be reproduced consistently, Kvadrat were prepared to go to the lengths required to manufacture it. One of the designs from the first collection, *Shadow*, was a vast repeat intended to take advantage of new digital printing technology that could accommodate much larger patterns. When the ink used in the new digital process turned out not to be sufficiently light-fast, rather than dropping the design Kvadrat produced it using eight separate print screens. 'It would have taken ages, but that's something that I really admire, that they'd just do that,' says Boontje.

As well as being technically challenging, like many of Boontje's designs *Shadow* addresses the role of textiles in space and how they can move beyond a traditional, rather stiff function into something more adaptable and fluid. It is a large pattern, inspired in part by the branch tapping against the window in Hitchcock's masterpiece of shadowplay *Rebecca*; dark shapes appear on the textile in various degrees of focus, suggesting branches and blooms silhouetted on thin fabric in moonlight. Created using hand drawings that were blurred in Photoshop, *Shadow* alludes to an imaginary light source; it diffuses the focus of a space, making

it appear more relaxing. 'People look around the room to see where the shadow is coming from,' explains Boontje.

Other designs – *100 Years* and *Eternal Summer* – are decorated using fine laser cuts into light-blocking textiles, creating a kind of embroidery with light. In daylight they register as white with a dark pattern; at night, dark with a white pattern; and they again create a dappled lighting effect that feeds the design through the rest of the space and which changes over the course of the day, moving with the light.

With these, and patterns such as *Heaven Scent* (which has a double-length serpentine repeat) and *Elements*, Boontje creates designs in two dimensions that will function in quite a particular way when transformed into three-dimensional objects. These two upholstery patterns escape the rigid grid to bring in an organic sensibility – they don't register as pattern but as ornament, and have what William Morris referred to as a 'satisfying mystery' which springs from the concealment of their geometric order. In using laser-cut curtains to create patterns with light, Boontje also re-casts ornamentation as an architectural element – subverting and softening the featureless surfaces of most modern interiors and breaking up the edges of the space.

'Be cautious of over-ornamenting your houses and your lives with cheap unenduring prettiness; have as few things as you can, for you may be sure that simplicity is the foundation of all worthy art; be sure that whatever ornament you have is proper and reasonable for the sort of life you want to lead, and don't be led by the nose by fashion into having things you don't want.'
– William Morris, *Textile Fabrics*, 1884

Strongly associated with the coloured, unadorned textiles used in the upholstery of Functionalist furni-ture of the twentieth century, Kvadrat's decision to move deeper into the arena of pattern was not uncon-troversial. The clean lines and colours of the modern movement and the Scandinavian furniture styles of the mid century had, 50 years after their first blossom-ing, become firmly lodged in popular mainstream taste. By the 1990s, IKEA was running mass-media advertisements exhorting customers to 'Chuck out your Chintz'; the clean, unadorned look, so modern in the mid century, had become, by the century's end, the default style for European and North American domestic interiors.

Boontje's rise to prominence in the early Noughties was part of the shift into a new era in design aesthetics,

Right: Tord Boontje, *Eternal Summer*, 2005
Facing page: Tord Boontje, *Elements*, 2009
Following pages, left: Tord Boontje, *100 Years*, 2009
Following pages, right: Tord Boontje, *Heaven Scent*, 2005

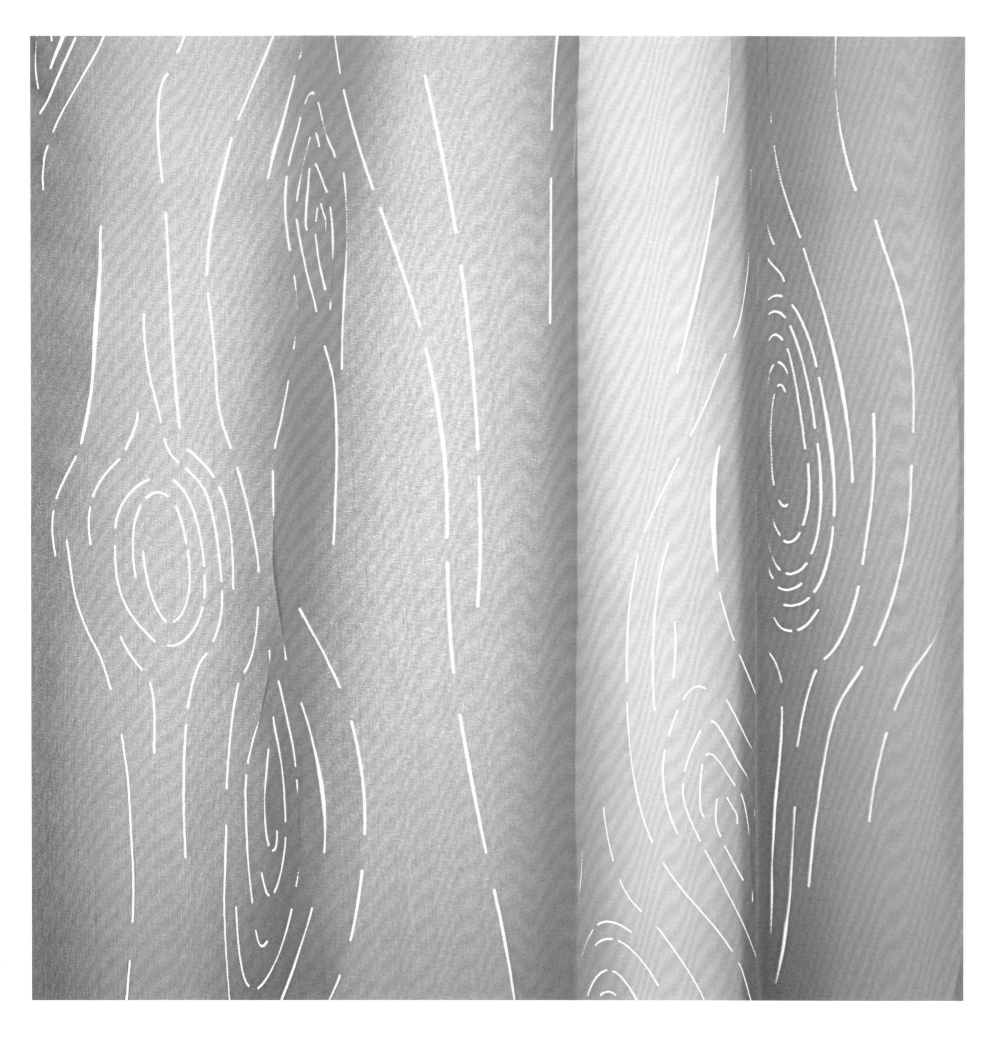

Screenprinting *Shadow* in production at Mitlödi, Switzerland
Facing page: Tord Boontje, preliminary test for new collection of curtains inspired by sunsets
Following page: Interior of the Tord Boontje shop, London

one moving away from the flood of tyrannical, pared-back 'tastefulness' towards a greater embrace of decoration and ornament. For Kvadrat, working in collaboration with Boontje marked an important and symbolic evolution, a long-term commitment to push the company in fresh directions that could develop and grow in complement to their existing output.

'It's an important part [of what we do] to be curious and to know what's coming up and going on,' explains Anne Jørgensen. 'We are always looking for new things, but it needs to be the right quality. We always need this feeling of doing something that is interesting not only for the next 24 hours, but that can stay for a while.'

For both parties, working together would involve negotiating the fuzzy line between innovation and fashion. Kvadrat's reputation rested to an extent on creating fabrics of enduring quality – however beautifully something is made, if it is already the height of fashion at the moment of manufacture then its physical durability is moot. Fashion can translate into a short shelf life, and ornamented things with a strong personality are afflicted most acutely. A very recognizable pattern can become over-exposed much more quickly than a particular shade of green.

Boontje describes the varied responses to the first collection as a learning experience. 'Some fabrics were picked up by a lot of manufacturers and used very strongly. Fritz Hansen, for example, did an Arne Jacobsen chair in *Heaven Scent*, which was really surprising. It was very popular very quickly, then everybody had seen it, so it disappeared. Whereas other things like *Shadow* and the computer-generated pattern *Nectar* are still going. *Wilderness*, the big hand drawing, is out of production already – it was maybe too classic.'

'You cannot well go wrong so long as you avoid commonplace, and keep somewhat on the daylight side of nightmare.'
–William Morris, *Some Hints on Pattern Designing*, 1881

When Boontje and other ornamental designers started coming to public attention around the turn of the century, comparisons with William Morris seemed omnipresent. One wonders what Morris, an avowed classicist and defender of ancient and vernacular architecture, would have made of Boontje's fascination with the beauty of the commonplace – his broken-glass patterns, and plans for curtains made in the graduated colours of sunset – and his tendency to embrace the nightmare rather than skirt politely around it. One imagines that he certainly would have admired the younger designer's industriousness, as well as his social awareness and roving curiosity.

Since the start of his collaborations with Kvadrat, Boontje's workspace has moved from an attic studio in south London, to a vast workshop in the forest in France, to an airy shop and studio space in Charlotte Road, in the heart of London's design district. The mingling of the selling and making spaces underlines his deep involvement in hand-worked objects and in shifting, informal experimentation – the downstairs gallery shows products that are still in progress, pieces that he and his team are tinkering with even as they are displayed for sale. Manufacture is not hidden; design consumers are instead invited to think about the development of objects and the way that they are made.

Boontje has a continued commitment to and affection for his work. Pieces are on display in the shop from every stage in his career, and he often goes back to revisit old ideas. He's making cherry-pip jewellery again (with pips supplied by his lemonade-making aunt), but now they're interspersed with juice-bright crystals. There are scary, pretty shadows everywhere, and little animals, and the suggestion of branches. The Kvadrat textiles are there as well, of course, taking their own place in his personal and design history.

Zoë Ryan

Ronan & Erwan Bouroullec's
quiet design revolution

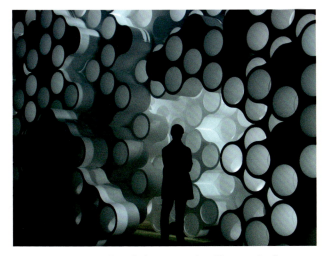

Ronan & Erwan Bouroullec, *Cloud*, 2002 (produced by Cappellini)

Ronan & Erwan Bouroullec, *Algues*, 2004 (produced by Vitra)

Paris-based designers Erwan and Ronan Bouroullec take a principled approach to designing furniture and products, yet their output is anything but rigid and inflexible. Interested in creating work with an integral logic, they develop projects with acute attention to striking the right balance between the formal and functional elements of a design, as well as determining the appropriate manufacturing process and material choices. 'For me, an object is a complex alchemy of details,' explains Ronan, the elder of the two brothers. 'Every component – the delicacy of a curve, the thickness of the material, an object's comfort – is fundamental. It's like writing a text message. You need to find the right words. It's the same with an object. The quality of its expression is key.' Rather than create work for a given environment, however, the Bouroullecs have become adept at carefully generating designs that can fit different situations and requirements. Whether designing products, furniture or work on a more environmental scale, the brothers are driven by an interest in imbuing their output with multiple qualities that provide a variety of functional, spatial and aesthetic outcomes to suit different needs. As Erwan confirms, 'We are afraid of an idea that is set in time and space and inflexible to change over time.' 'We are interested in diversity and complexity,' says Ronan. The result is

elegant designs that command a space without overpowering their surroundings.

It is the apparent dichotomy of their approach, which is at once tailored and open-ended, that has defined their practice since they founded their studio together in 1999. Although their portfolio of projects has grown steadily over the years, with work for an international array of companies including Cappellini, Vitra, Magis and Kvadrat, as well as Paris-based Galerie Kreo, the Bouroullecs' working methods remain the same. They are steadfast in their desire to retain a hands-on approach that requires them to oversee every project in an effort to exert maximum control over their production. Sitting side by side at one end of their workshop-like studio, and aided by a handful of talented assistants who reside at the opposite end of the linear space, the brothers continue to sketch and make physical models that enhance the intellectual rigor of their work and ensure that a project is realised to its highest potential.

In addition to furniture and products, the Bouroullecs have become increasingly recognised for a more loosely categorised set of projects that could be described as room hardware, which works on a variety of scales, from wall hangings to room dividers to entire enclosures. Most significant is the work they

have produced with Kvadrat, with whom they have developed a close working relationship over the past six years that has pushed both their practices in new directions, with innovative results. As Erwan acknowledges, 'Kvadrat came at the perfect time for us, when we were beginning to research work that was between a wall and a piece of furniture.' This line of inquiry began early on in their practice, with projects such as *Joyn*, made for Vitra in 2002: a modular system for the office with communal desks that users can customise with slot-on partitions and other accessories to vary their degree of privacy as well as enhance functionality. The *Cloud* bookshelf, produced in 2002 for Cappellini, is also a system of elements, this time cubbyhole-like units that can be stacked on top of one another to form a large-scale bookshelf or room divider. As Ronan says, 'We split our approach in two ways. On the one hand we have been making furniture like small-scale architecture, as an efficient way of creating space. On the other hand we have been making work that defines walls.' In 2004, the Bouroullecs also developed for Vitra the popular *Algues*: plastic versions of plant-like forms that can be clipped together to create a dense screen reminiscent of wild flora and fauna. The *Alcove Sofa*, a high-backed chair launched in 2007 also for Vitra, similarly aims to define an interior

Facing page: Ronan & Erwan Bouroullec, research models for *North Tiles*, 2006
Below: Ronan & Erwan Bouroullec, research model for Mudam installation, 2006

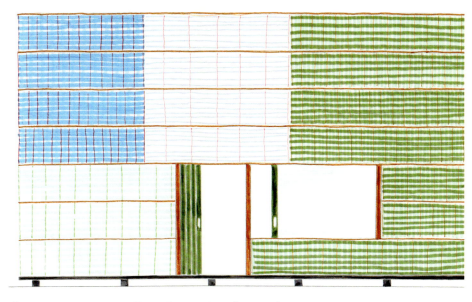

Above: Ronan & Erwan Bouroullec, preliminary sketch for Kvadrat's Stockholm showroom, 2006
Facing page: Ronan & Erwan Bouroullec, *North Tiles*, 2006 (installed in Kvadrat's Stockholm showroom)

environment and carve out an area of more personal or private space.

What is particularly interesting about the relationship with Kvadrat, however, is that rather than working with the company's core competency to create a new textile design, the Bouroullecs imaginatively proposed drawing on Kvadrat's existing catalogue of fabric as the basis for an entirely new type of product. Fabric and textiles have been an essential aspect of Erwan and Ronan's interests since early on in their careers. As fresh-faced designers, they would borrow textile samples from Kvadrat, a manufacturer they continue to admire for its strong point of view, high-quality product and broad spectrum of colour choices. Increasingly, the brothers have come to understand the potential inherent in textiles to determine an interior and create a welcoming environment in which to live. According to Erwan, their interests have increasingly developed in this direction as they seek 'new solutions that can compete with drywall in the creation of space. We want to come up with real solutions that people can use that don't involve plasterboard and paint.'

These ideas were tested to their fullest when the Bouroullecs were invited in to design Kvadrat's Stockholm showroom, which opened in 2006. After much debate and dragging of feet based on their aversion to creating permanent interior environments that can't be modified over time, Erwan and Ronan returned to Anders Byriel, CEO and son of its founder, almost a year after the initial proposal. They presented him with the seed of an idea that could on the one hand be used to create a dynamic interior space for the showroom and that had the potential to morph and change over time, yet on the other could be developed into a product to be sold through the company. From here, Byriel took a leap of faith, and the innovative idea for a system of tiles made from Kvadrat fabric was born.

Entitled *North Tiles*, the flexible elements, which are made from a foam core covered in Kvadrat textile, slot together and can be configured to create everything from a decorative wall hanging to a freestanding partition. The tiles function similarly to slate tiles on a roof, overlapping at the top and bottom to create dense arrangements of colour and material. Although *North Tiles* immediately caught the attention of the design world, they proved difficult to produce and expensive to buy, and were therefore not a commercial success. However, perceiving the potential of the idea, the Bouroullecs were determined to generate a new design, based on similar principles, that was more user-friendly and less costly. After a long process of development, in 2009, *Clouds* were introduced. Although more complex in construction, the irregular shape of the fabric tile was made easier to manufacture and assemble and has therefore proven to be a commercial hit.

The *Clouds* tiles stand out for their three-dimensional quality, which allows for an infinite range of possible arrangements. Used as ceiling tiles, freestanding elements, or adhered to the wall, they generate a soft surface that absorbs sound and diffuses light. Made from a compressed wool substrate, the individual flexible components are held together with an elemental, easy-to-use system of rubber bands that are not only a functional but also an aesthetic element. Visible from the front, they delineate the individual tiles, enhancing their sculptural appearance. Drawing on Kvadrat's portfolio of fabrics, the *Clouds* are made using two of their core textiles: *Divina* and *Tempo* created respectively by Finn Sködt, and Frans Dijkmeijer with Georgina Wright.

Reacting more like felt than a woven fabric, *Divina* proved ideal for more complex geometries of form. In addition, the fabric can be cut to size without fraying, therefore making stitching unnecessary, and limiting the number of steps in the manufacturing process.

Clouds are exemplary of the Bouroullecs' methods. Rather than *grands projets*, the brothers prefer to reinterpret quotidian essentials, updating them for

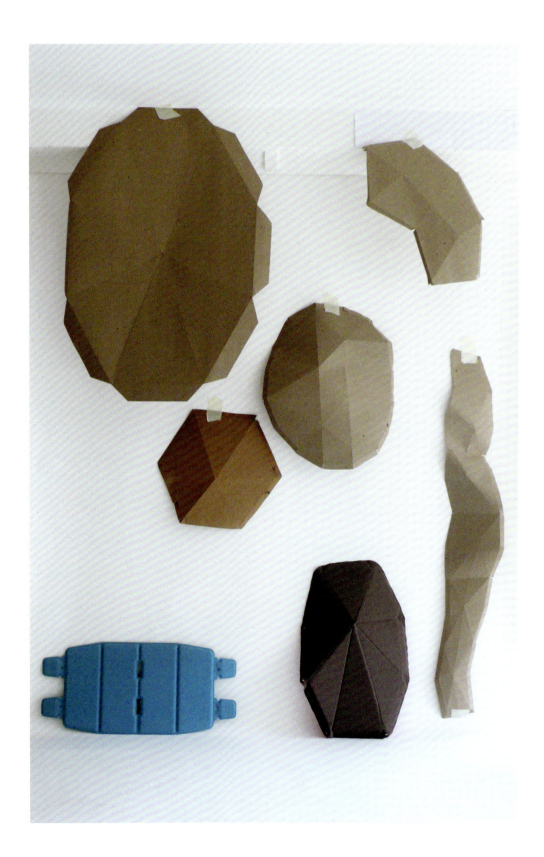

Ronan & Erwan Bouroullec, research models for *Clouds*, 2009
Facing page: Ronan & Erwan Bouroullec, *Clouds*, 2009
(studio installation view)

Ronan & Erwan Bouroullec, *Parasol Lumineux*, 2001 (produced by Galerie Kreo)

Verner Panton, *Living Tower*, 1968/69 (produced by Vitra/ Herman Miller)

Joe Colombo, *Rotoliving* and *Cabriolet-bed*, 1969 (produced by Sormani)

contemporary times. Signature work such as the afore-mentioned *Joyn*, *Algues*, *Cloud* bookshelf and *Alcove Sofa*, as well as the *Clouds* tiles, emphasize the Bouroullecs' interest in creating work with hybrid properties that encourages user interaction.

Correlations can be found between the Bouroullecs' interests and those of an earlier generation of designers such as Achille and Pier Giacomo Castiglioni and Enzo Mari, as well as Charles and Ray Eames and Robin and Lucienne Day, who were particularly active in this way in the 1950s and 60s. These designers emphasized the value of objects that have become subsumed into our daily lives, their origins forgotten or taken for granted. They looked to emphasise the notion that design is not only about formal and functional considerations, but also about ideas through which users engage with a work on a universal level. Like their predecessors, the Bouroullecs inventively seek to rethink otherwise standard domestic objects, as well as introduce entirely new ones for everyday use.

Critical to the Bouroullecs' unique methodology is their aptitude for creating designs that have multi-functional qualities, that can perform as part of a system or network of elements, on a range of scales, and transform spaces. As Erwan confirms, 'We enjoy creating modular elements that can confront the strict

geometries of a space.' This mindset is reflected in proj-ects made for mass production, as well as in commis-sions made as limited editions such as *Cabane* and *Parasol Lumineux*, both conceived in 2001 for Galerie Kreo in Paris. *Cabane* resembles a cross between a football goal and a gazebo and provides a frame for a lounge area or play space within an existing interior. *Parasol Lumineux*, which works like a café-table umbrella, is a large-scale standard lamp that acts as a frame for the space below. Both designs rethink conventional objects for the home. What makes the *North Tiles* and *Clouds* stand out, however, is the numerous possibilities they offer for defining spaces with various configurations and further conflating distinctions between an object and an environment.

The Bouroullecs' interest in modular systems and designs that have the capacity to adapt to suit the user follows a long lineage of work by pioneers that include George Nelson, Joe Colombo, Verner Panton and Nanna Ditzel, who worked in this way from the late 1940s into the 1970s. Nelson's *Basic Cabinet Series* from 1946, designed for office spaces; Ditzel's *Living Dock* seating from 1961; and Panton's *Living Tower* and Colombo's more all-encompassing designs such as his *Habitat of the Future*, both from 1969, borrowed references from across disciplines and also mined

contemporary culture for ideas, creatively reinterpret-ing conventional designs for live, work and play spaces that questioned notions of formality and allowed for user customisation. However, unlike the emphasis on total design, which was being explored at this time in a desire for total control over every aspect of a space as a way to exercise the designer's influence, the Bouroul-lecs prefer to create work in which the user is encour-aged to determine their own outcomes as an inherent aspect of the design. This is especially the case with the *Clouds* for Kvadrat. 'We wanted a design that would go quite wild in a space,' says Erwan. 'You have to trust the process, even though you can't completely control the form. The tiles aren't symmetrical, there is no left or right, it is an organic form and relies on an organic process of building up the elements intuitively.' Like much of the Bouroullecs' work, the shape of the tiles was inspired by the organising systems of plants and other forms found in nature. However, unlike some of their contemporaries who might prefer to use a para-metric approach to determine the complex forms of the tiles and detect the number of possible configura-tions, the Bouroullecs favour an analogue process and sculpted the design by hand, using models and mock-ups to achieve the desired effect. Even they aren't aware of all the possible outcomes, preferring to be surprised.

Ronan & Erwan Bouroullec, plant structure drawing, research for
Clouds and other organically inspired designs, 2008

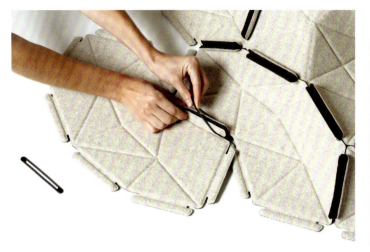

Ronan & Erwan Bouroullec, *Clouds*, 2009 (detail, elastic band fixings)

Jean Prouvé, *La Maison Tropicale*, 1949/51 (Brazzaville)

In addition to their formal properties, what makes *Clouds* even more visionary, though, is their simplicity. Understanding the increasing loss of handicraft skills in contemporary culture, the Bouroullecs have created a design in which no cutting or stitching is required and therefore there is no possibility for error. 'We see our work as dealing with a Darwinism or evolutionary process of function,' says Ronan. 'We take clues from contemporary culture in order to create work that is responsive to new changes and needs. People are slowly losing the skill of working with a hammer or a brush. We therefore need to create designs that do not rely on previously gained knowledge or tools that people no longer have in their homes. We collect the general wisdom of people and determine designs that speak to this.'

As previously noted, what results is a design that functions as a piece of hardware. Users can manipulate the *Clouds* tiles for their own uses without the need for specific tools or know-how to construct designs whose configuration is never the same twice. Rather than conceal the method of construction, however, the Bouroullecs have made it an essential feature. The rubber bands which hold each tile together are kept visible rather than hidden away, revealing the simplistic construction methods and making the

object as inviting to interact with as possible.

These aesthetic, yet at the same time functional decisions relate directly to those adhered to by designers working in the early part of the twentieth century such as Jean Prouvé, a Frenchman known for his interests in engineering designs whose appearance reflected the process of their creation as an inherent part of the design. Projects such as his prototypical house *La Maison Tropicale*, of which three examples were produced between 1949 and 1951, illustrate an interest in designing buildings that could be manufactured economically and that could easily be erected and disassembled, made from modular components and industrial materials. His ideas influenced generations of designers who followed, including the British designer Jasper Morrison, whom the Bouroullecs credit as inspiration. Morrison, who rose to fame in the 1990s for furniture such as the *Low Pad* chair for Cappellini and *Air Chair* for Magis (both 1999), is known for refined yet thoughtful solutions to everyday domestic objects. Rather than seducing the user with intricacy, Morrison relies on a straightforward – yet nonetheless inventive – approach as a way to rethink standard typologies of form and function. Ronan and Erwan adhere to a similar ideology. 'Our designs are as much a conversation between the manufacturing

process of a piece as they are about the function of a design,' says Ronan. 'Our work is often made up of component parts that together take on a strong character. We therefore need to make sure that these components are expressive of the manufacturing and construction of our designs as a legible forum for expressing form and function. It is not a question of perfection but of doing things correctly.'

Their pro-functionalist approach is evident in another piece of hardware for Kvadrat: this time a device for hanging curtains, launched in 2013. At first one wonders why such a humble domestic product might interest the brothers. However, they assert that no design is too inconsequential, and instead it seems that hanging curtains has become something of a personal project for the pair, who both have young children. And yet creating a simple, yet elegant solution to introduce Kvadrat curtain fabrics in the home, which can be cut to fit without the need to be hemmed, proved to be an unexpected challenge, and found them deriving inspiration from another ingenious, yet little-celebrated object: the guitar peg, used to tighten strings. Borrowing from the same principle, the Bouroullecs conceived of a support system whereby a length of super-strong cord is held taut between two winding mechanisms attached to the wall. The curtain

Ronan & Erwan Bouroullec, research models for *Ready Made Curtain* for Kvadrat, 2013

Ronan & Erwan Bouroullec, research models for *Ready Made Curtain*, 2013
Facing page: Ronan & Erwan Bouroullec, *Ready Made Curtain*, 2013
(details of the mechanism)

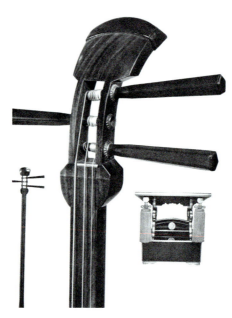

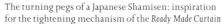

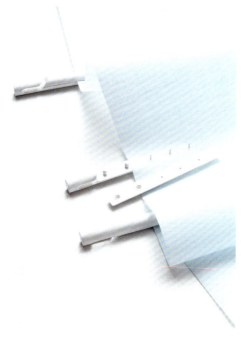

The turning pegs of a Japanese Shamisen: inspiration for the tightening mechanism of the *Ready Made Curtain*

Ready Made Curtain (detail), fixing the pegs

is attached to the cord using custom-designed plastic pegs. This kit of parts allows users to hang fabrics (a choice between three non-woven colourways and three woollen colourways) quickly and with as little fuss as possible in front of windows, as room dividers, or even as wall hangings for visual effect. 'At first it seems trivial,' says Erwan, 'but hanging fabric can have a real impact in a room, whether that's on the quality of the light or by introducing softness and texture.' Since 2012, Erwan and Ronan have also been working with Kvadrat on a parallel project exploring the mechanism of roller blinds.

Having shown a flair for revolutionising objects at a molecular level for Kvadrat, Erwan and Ronan have also been keen to demonstrate their dexterity as designers on a larger scale. In addition to designing, in 2009, Kvadrat's Copenhagen showroom, which makes generous use of their *Clouds* tiles for carving out individual areas and providing different atmospheres, in 2011 they were invited to create an installation using Kvadrat textiles for the London Design Festival within the Victoria and Albert Museum. Given free rein, the designers elected to install a landscape of fabric in the famed Raphael Gallery. *Textile Field*, as its name suggests, functioned like a public space in which visitors to the museum could congregate, even lie

down, to view the seven towering cartoons, which were painted by Raphael in 1515–16. The 240 sqm environment, made up of individual sections of foam covered in muted shades of *Hallingdal* fabric, tilted slightly upward on either side, creating a gently sloping surface for visitors to rest upon, resembling a network of ploughed fields whose complex layout is only ever fully comprehended when viewed from above. The colours of the individual sections were determined as a means of guiding the eye across the surface and thereby encouraging user engagement. 'We wanted to create something that was akin to a public park,' says Ronan, 'where children and adults would be at the same level and weren't afraid to have an opinion about these beautiful works whose origin seems far removed from our time, and the soaring volume of the room makes people even more distanced from them.' The piece was reinstalled a month later, in October 2011, as part of the Bouroullecs' monographic exhibition at the Pompidou-Metz, and then again in 2012 at the Museum of Contemporary Art in Chicago and at Les Arts Décoratifs in Paris in 2013. As with much of their earlier work, critical to *Textile Field* was the potential of the design to carve out communal gathering space, bringing people together to share experiences.

As their work attests, Ronan and Erwan have an amazing capacity to identify latent areas of development that, when harnessed, drive inventive and often unanticipated outcomes. Bent on achieving work that is intuitive and produced in response to human needs and activities, the brothers are adept at rethinking the fundamental elements of daily life, positing alternative solutions. With their output for Kvadrat, they have been able to work outside the company, rather than as in-house designers, with the freedom to reflect on the company's strengths and determine designs that harness this potential. As Ronan notes, 'Kvadrat is like a very nice grocery store, rather than a huge supermarket. They don't try and do everything, but they understand what they do well.' Fearless in their combined approach, the Bouroullecs have found an ideal partner, and one that they recognise helps them stretch their minds in order to create projects that have the ability to confound expectation, as well as furthering the field of design on a micro, as well as a macro level.

Ronan & Erwan Bouroullec, *Ready Made Curtain*, 2013

Below and facing page: Ronan & Erwan Bouroullec, *Textile Field*, 2011 (installation, Raphael Gallery, Victoria and Albert Museum, London)
Following pages: Ronan & Erwan Bouroullec, models and mechanism tests for a roller blind prototype for Kvadrat, 2013

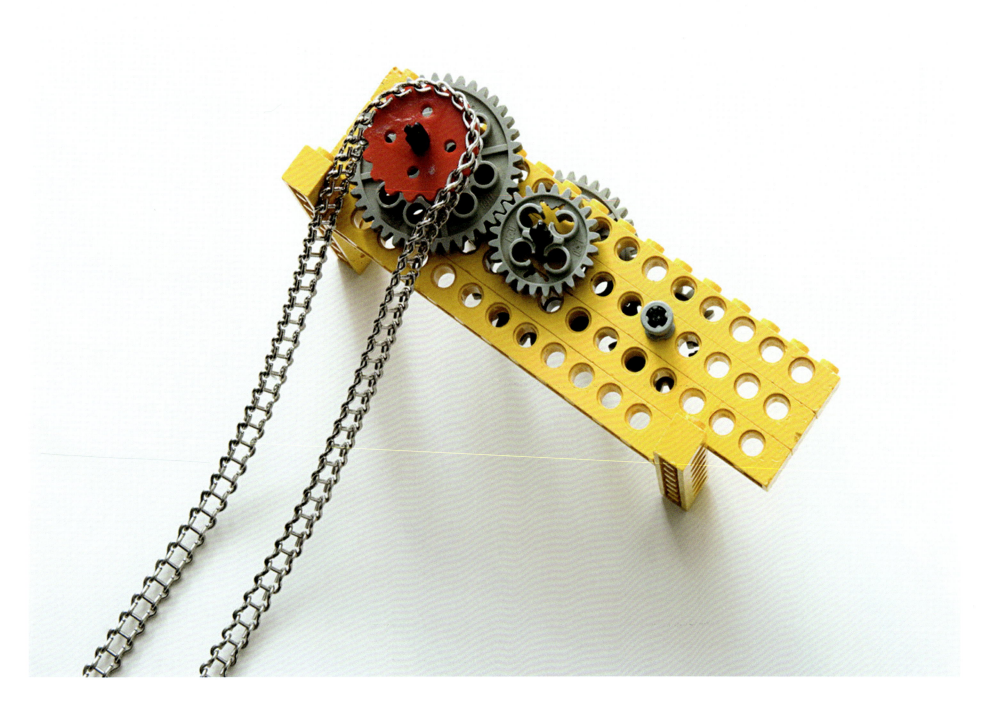

Gledhill, Wooltex and Mitlödi
Joël Tettamanti

The Swiss photographer Joël Tettamanti is engaged in
an ongoing project to create a photographic portrait
of Kvadrat from the ground up. Journeying around the
world to document the gathering of wool, weaving of
cloth, dyeing, printing and processing, he builds up
portraits of working communities and the natural
and industrial landscapes they inhabit.

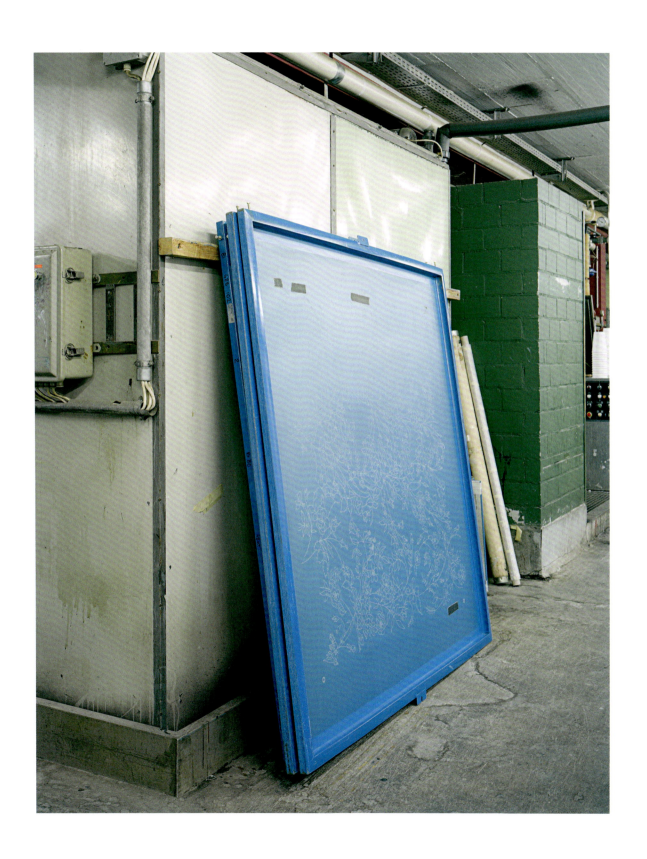

Sevil Peach
with Hettie Judah

The resurrection of fabric
in architecture

Sevil Peach, rolls of *Divina* fabric from Kvadrat awaiting use at the Vitra Design Museum Summer Workshops, Boisbuchet, France, 2008

In 2002 Oscar Tusquets Blanca curated an exhibition about staircases at the Centre de Cultura Contemporània de Barcelona. Entitled *Rèquiem per l'escala* (Requiem for the staircase), it was about the history of staircases and how they have steadily lost their importance; escalators and elevators have now supplanted the staircase's celebratory, central role as a unifying element of buildings.

This idea of requiem made me think about the current role of textiles within architecture and interiors. In recent years taste has moved away from the use of textiles as a space-enhancing element in favour of a more pared-back look; at most, architects use textile elements only as a final, accessorising touch, a mere soft furnishing component, rather then an integral part of architecture. I believe that despite the shift in tastes, the tactility of textiles, the use of colour, texture and fluidity, can significantly enhance and transform the way we feel and use spaces.

It is worth acknowledging that discussion surrounding the use of textiles is also a gendered one, bedevilled by a fear of perceived feminine connotations that has perhaps left this a subject too little studied. As Marianne Eggler notes in her study of Mies Van der Rohe and Lilly Reich's interiors in the *Tugendhat Villa*, 'Under close analysis, their hanging curtain partitions (which have until now avoided critical scrutiny, perhaps due to their inferior status as 'soft' furnishings) conceal considerably more ideology than their elegant velvets and silks normally communicate.'

Fabrics have a complex relationship with architecture. For nomadic peoples, they provide shelter that is flexible, lightweight and portable; in ancient buildings they offer insulation and privacy; they can give softness to a space; they can be a defining feature to create spaces and they can help control the flow and quality of light and sound. I feel that there is a need to resurrect and rethink the use of fabric within architecture.

In 2008 and 2009, I ran a series of workshops for the Vitra Design Museum's Summer School in Boisbuchet, France, to examine the potential role of fabric in design, using over 1,000m of different textiles, in a variety of colours, donated by Kvadrat. The aims were to encourage participants to explore, understand, and feel the nature of textiles and colour and to open their minds to its potential applications. The experiments conducted in the workshops were as much an educational process for me as they were for the participants involved. I was dealing with fabric in a completely different way, on a completely different scale and in a very different place to that which I was used to. This opened up new channels of thought for me, some of which have already been explored in our studio. One way or the other, these free-spirited experiments find their way into our projects. They have also prompted me to think more about the wider architectural use of textiles and what other seeds of resurrection there are out there.

The workshops

The focus of the workshops was to experiment with how we could use fabric as an architectural tool, and how it could manipulate, influence and change our perception of space and place.

In 2008 we experimented with the fluidity of the fabrics, and the complexity of colour, using all 56 different tones of Kvadrat's *Divina* range of fabrics. In 2009 we had a tighter colour palette and focused on fabric as planes and surfaces within archetypal forms used as the basic building block for installations, enclosures, sculptures and social events.

Our investigations with textiles fell roughly into four areas. Firstly, examining the role and impact of colour. Secondly, looking at how textiles might be used to create an architectural form. Thirdly, exploring the masking and technical impact of textiles and how they influenced light, appearance and acoustics; and finally

Facing page: Sevil Peach, students in coloured cloaks, Vitra Design Museum Summer Workshops, Boisbuchet, France, 2008
Below: Sevil Peach, fabrics as planes, Vitra Design Museum Summer Workshops, Boisbuchet, France, 2008

Sevil Peach, curtain-walled project room, 2011 (Vitra office, Weil am Rhein)

Petra Blaisse, *Re-set*, 2012 (Dutch pavilion, Venice Architecture Biennale)

an investigation into the way textiles can influence our experience of places, spaces and people, and the capacity they have to create spectacle – the 'Wow!' factor.

Colour

Prejudice surrounding colour is complex. In part people have a learned response – they will have been taught not to wear certain combinations of colour, or that certain colours are ugly or vulgar. In part there is sensitivity to the 'appropriate' use of colour. A business environment traditionally dictated sombre and conservative tones of black, grey and navy; bright colours, by contrast, might be read as frivolous, feminine or even emotional.

During the 2008 workshops we made up 56 cloaks in different colours for the participants to wear in an attempt to overcome their prejudices. We worked to create groups of colour to show how the impact and connotations can change in context. The colours selected as unattractive are often the ones that make up the most beautiful views in nature, as became apparent when we created a group that attempted to reproduce the colours of the Boisbuchet landscape and saw that it overwhelmingly contained colours that had previously been identified as ugly by participants earlier on. There is no such thing as an ugly colour.

Colour in a woven textile is very different to flat colour on a painted wall. It has a depth of field and texture that really draws you in; it's seductive. A solid wall reflects and can push you away; textile on the other hand tends to pull you in. Use of fabric and colour can also change the mood of a space quite strongly, creating soft retreat spaces or areas that feel very energised, peaceful or intense.

The flip side of prejudice is that people tend to have a very personal relationship with colours, which they feel can communicate something very particular about them, their company or their brand. We have used a strong and varied palette of coloured textiles in our design of co-working offices for Spaces in the historic *Red Elephant* building in The Hague. The intention is to provide the members with a variety of places to meet or work in, allowing them to choose those which they feel best reflect their mood and needs. We have achieved this not only through a variety of design installations but also through the selection of fabric, colour and furniture.

Of course, in the end the choice of colour is a question of what is appropriate; strong colours are not always right for the space – a really large fabric volume might call for something more neutral that allows it to harmonise easily with its surroundings.

Form

For the 2009 workshops, we focused on primary colours and selected six colours to work with. We limited the exercise to one archetypal form: a square. At the beginning of the workshop all the participants rolled out the textiles by hand and familiarised themselves with their differing natures. They then had to stretch the fabrics across two dozen 2.2m square frames. These frames were much like the stretchers used by artists, but the textiles that we were using were more pliable and giving than canvas; understanding the particular behaviour of textiles when used as a construction material became an important part of this exercise.

The light, flexible nature of textile lends itself to the creation of temporary forms within a space. In the 1960s, the French designer Pierre Paulin created a new interior at the Elysée Palace for President Georges Pompidou that used modern stretch fabrics over a metal frame. This lightweight structure-within-a- structure left Joseph-Eugène Lacroix's original nineteenth-century décor untouched, while providing Pompidou with a modern living space more in keep-ing with his tastes.

In the office environments we design, we often use stretched fabric on the walls and the ceilings, like

Sevil Peach, interior of *Spaces, The Red Elephant*, 2013 (The Hague, Netherlands)

Sevil Peach, fabric-lined study rooms, 2011 (Vitra office, Weil am Rhein)

Sevil Peach, fabric-lined study boxes, 2011 (Vitra office, Weil am Rhein)

Shigeru Ban, *Naked House*, 2000 (Kawagoe, Japan)

Sou Fujimoto, *House N*, 2008 (Oita City, Japan)

Kvadrat's *Soft Cells* panels, both to introduce colour and for acoustic insulation. We also often use very large curtains architecturally as space dividers, to create adaptable and flexible zones within a larger space.

Using tracked curtains in place of walls allows the nature of a structure to change rapidly and profoundly, from one with multiple divisions into an opened out space, from translucent to opaque and even from there to not there. We are currently working on a project in Shanghai which uses two tracked 6m-high curtains to create a huge lantern-like form at the heart of the building's communal space. Ordinarily the curtains will be sheer and provide two rooms for playing table tennis in the company's dining area. Thicker curtains can be used on parallel tracks to block sound and light, transforming them into private meeting rooms. The adjoining section of the curtains can be removed to create a larger contained space as a lecture hall, or the curtains can be pulled back completely to open out the whole space for large events. You can't do this with a wall.

The Dutch designer Petra Blaisse played with similar ideas in her *Re-Set* installation at the 2012 Venice Architecture Biennale, for which she sent vast lengths of fabric shuttling around tracks in a large space. Using panels that were variously brightly coloured, reflective and transparent, the giant kinetic curtain created changing forms, spaces and atmospheres. A regular collaborator with Rem Koolhaas' OMA practice, Petra has used movable curtains to create temporary, adaptable forms in architectural projects including an auditorium at Harvard University and a new interior for the Haus der Kunst in Munich.

Fabric as a mask and technical intervention

In 2008 several groups from the workshop looked at the idea of textile as an environmental modifier, discovering how interiors could be completely changed by the use of fabric and colour. Taking occupation of an empty coal store and bakery on the Boisbuchet estate, the spaces were entirely wrapped from floor to ceiling in fabric of a single colour. This dramatically altered the acoustics, and the spaces immediately became retreats and meditative places. Upon entering these formerly dead and abandoned sites, one felt wrapped up and safe; serene in the beautiful and tranquil textile-lined space.

The next year, participants were asked to use their stretched-fabric panels to create three-dimensional shapes such as triangles, boxes and tunnels in different colours. One of the most succesful interventions of the workshop was the modification of the long commu-

nal dining tables by enclosing them with a number of masking canopies that transformed this functional outdoor space into an 'event'. It was remarkable to see the effect these canopies had on those at the meal; people gathered under their favourite colour, and dinner that evening became the longest and most sociable of the week.

In the refurbishment of Vitra's offices in Weil am Rhein in 2010 we further explored the acoustic and meditative aspects of fabric as an architectural component by using the findings from this workshop. We designed a series of stretched-fabric meeting boxes that were inserted into walls as well as stand-alone smaller individual work boxes, offering the employees a place of retreat or a discrete concentration space within the open-plan office. These comfortable, informal workspaces allow employees to work quietly on their own or with others. Functioning in a very similar way to the enclosures created in the workshop, the different colours of the fabric-clad boxes provoke different reactions from those using them – workers using the office find themselves drawn to particular colours at different times and for particular purposes.

Used inside a building, textiles can be thought of as a soft inner shell, creating a cocoon-like space and sense of containment that can have particular impact

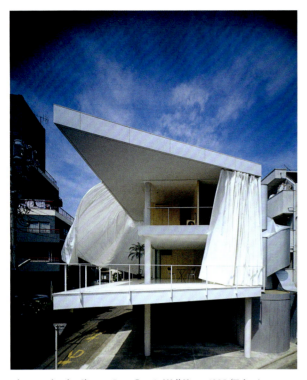

Above and right: Shigeru Ban, *Curtain Wall House*, 1995 (Tokyo)
Facing page: Sevil Peach, structural textile project, Vitra Design Museum
Summer Workshops, Boisbuchet, France, 2008

within relatively stark or industrial structures. This idea has been used with spectacular restraint in Sou Fujimoto's *House N* (2008), which has a very open, nested structure in which curtains divide the space and offer privacy. Textile creates an even more important shell within Shigeru Ban's radically stripped-back *Naked House* (2000), a long shed-like space in which personal rooms are replaced by open-sided cubicles on castors, and nylon curtains are used in place of interior walls.

The wow factor

Shigeru Ban has also used textiles to theatrical architectural effect in his *Curtain Wall House* (1995), in which a fluid white curtain is suspended to form a façade on two sides of the house between the second and third floors. The curtain takes the place of the sliding screens used in traditional Japanese architecture, and allows for a summer living space open to nature. The curtain wall can be enclosed in folding doors when insulation or privacy is desired.

In Boisbuchet we converted the three-sided enclosures used for the dining table mask into four-sided coloured cubes that were rolled, stacked, floated and turned into a variety of sculptural shapes within the landscape. Through manipulating the fabric

panels, we shaped and changed the experience of the places, spaces and people. We communicated this in the grounds of Boisbuchet by creating a visual spectacle for all attendees at the various workshops to interact with and quickly grasp the fundamental ideas being explored.

Textiles can create eye-catching punctuation within a space – at the Vitra offices and the office development in the *Red Elephant* building we have used spectacularly high curtains in place of doors in certain spaces. The height of the curtain indicates from some distance whether the room is in use. In a large open-plan area these tall, coloured fabric curtains help people to negotiate their way around the space – acting as markers/signifiers in the landscape.

Diener & Diener's *Swiss Pavilion* for the Frankfurt Book Fair in 1998 demonstrated the poetic nature of the use of fabric by creating sequential zones delineated by different colours within a suspended 6.5m-high volume. The architecture practice Caruso St John has also made spectacular use of fabric in the exhibition scenographies that it has created for the artist Thomas Demand. For his 2004 *Phototrophy* exhibition at the Kunsthaus Bregenz, Austria, they created a remotely controlled curtain of Kvadrat's *Divina* fabric on tracks that moved on an eight-minute loop, pausing for 59

seconds when it reached the correct configuration for a screening of the artist's film *Trick* (2004). For his 2009 exhibition at the Neue Nationalgalerie in Berlin, heavy wool curtains (in Kvadrat's *Tonica* fabric) were draped from floor to ceiling, dividing up Mies van der Rohe's light, airy, wall-less building into a series of vertical and horizontal planes to define spaces that are intimate, weighty and quiet. Thomas Demand's pictures were ingeniously hung from these curtains as if they were simply gallery walls.

Resurrection

The architectural use of textile has an environmental impact in the widest sense. It has a softening effect within a building, making it more acoustically gentle, modifying the light and temperature and adding a seductive, tactile element to the surfaces.

Textile also allows for new structures to be created within an existing environment that don't compete aggressively with the language created by the original architects. When appropriate, creating a soft, flexible textile structure within an already spectacular volume can be a more architecturally sympathetic way of adapting a space than inserting solid partitions. It is transformative in a positive way, allowing for the

creation of a modern element in an older space, or a softer element in a hard, industrial space.

Textile structures co-exist gently with what came before them. Like the living structures of the nomads, they are lightweight and flexible, easier to put in place and to remove, and thus well suited to the desire for living and working spaces to be constantly refreshed or changed as demand and fashion dictate.

Most designers currently use fabric as an accessory, an adornment, a finishing touch to the space they have already created, usually for the inevitable curtains for the windows, or for upholstery. By using fabric as one of the primary delineators of form and looking at it on a place-making scale rather than as a mere embellishment, the scope and possibilities for spaces, buildings and places can be taken to a completely different level.

Diener & Diener, *Guest of Honour* Swiss Pavilion for the Frankfurt Book Fair, 1998. Facing page: Caruso St John with Thomas Demand, exhibition design, 2009 (Neue Nationalgalerie, Berlin)

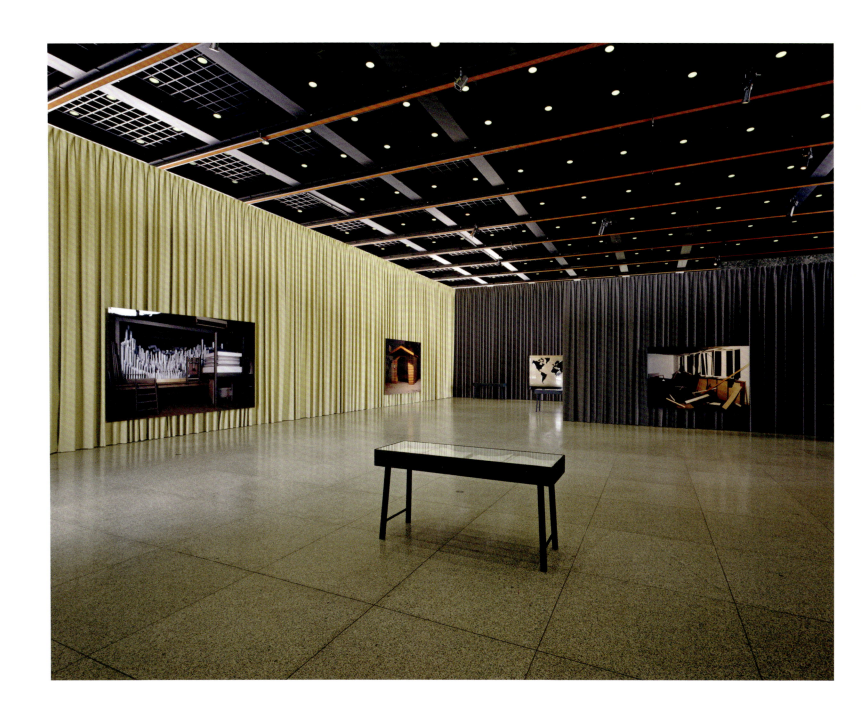

Sevil Peach, floor plan and fabric samples for *Spaces, The Red Elephant*, 2013 (The Hague, Netherlands)

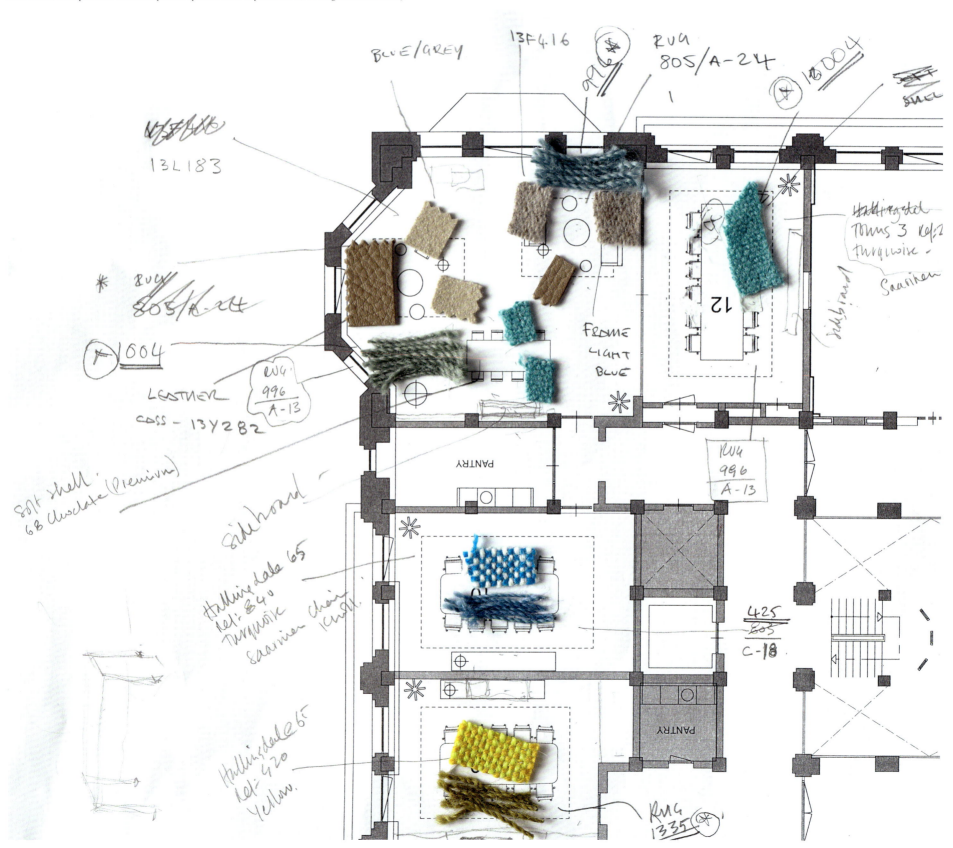

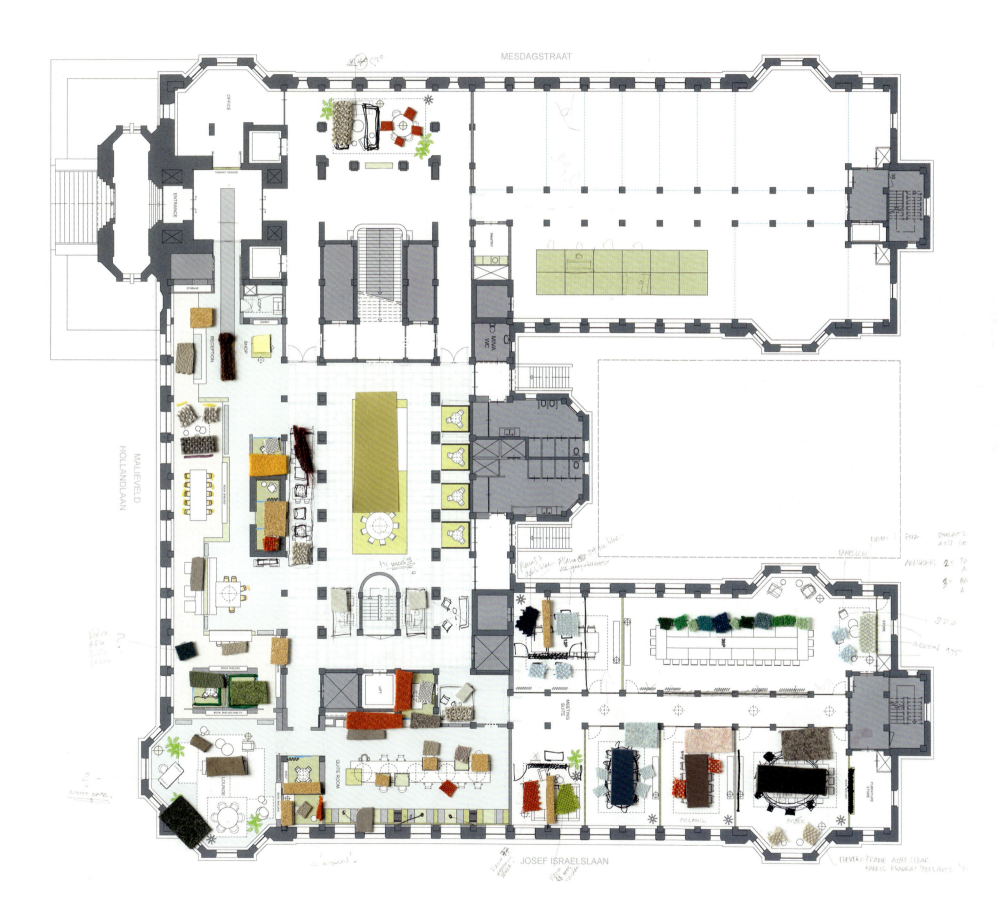

Sevil Peach, meeting rooms, *Spaces*, *The Red Elephant*, 2013 (The Hague, Netherlands)

Portfolio

Kvadrat design projects

As an extension of its close working relationship with the design world, Kvadrat has commissioned a series of inventive, large-scale installations.

Raw-Edges Design Studio *The Picnic*
The Picnic is a massive wood and textile installation created for Kvadrat's stand during the Stockholm Furniture Fair 2013. The installation is made up of a wooden structure, built from Douglas Fir from the Danish company Dinesen, and a textile structure, made up of 1,500 individual textile strips, which are suspended from the ceiling. Resembling vertical roof tiles, the strips were inspired by weeping willow trees, creating an intimate space within the big exhibition hall, and showing the subtle colours and textures of the fabric at close quarters.

Doshi Levien *The Wool Parade*
Created by the London-based design practice Doshi Levien, *The Wool Parade* is a choreography of 12 upholstered objects inspired by the avant-garde parties and architectural theatre costumes of the Bauhaus. Ambiguous geometric forms appear in various compositions, like marionettes, displaying an irreverent, playful and bold combination of fabrics. Moving around the suspended installation, the apparently abstract elements will, from various viewpoints, align momentarily to form a series of characters.

Patricia Urquiola *The Revolving Room*
In collaboration with Moroso, Kvadrat commissioned Patricia Urquiola to create an environmental installation in Moroso's Milan showroom for the 2013 Salone Internazionale del Mobile. *The Revolving Room* invites visitors into a space delineated by three-sided fabric panels that slowly revolve on individual axes. The evolving abstract scenography of the installation echoes the randomised graphic elements within the designs of Urquiola's first fabric collection for Kvadrat.

Patricia Urquiola, Giulio Ridolfo and BMW
The Dwelling Lab
In 2010, Kvadrat collaborated with Patricia Urquiola, Giulio Ridolfo and BMW to create a sculpture for the Salone Internazionale del Mobile in Milan. *The Dwelling Lab* is a radical interpretation of a BMW 5 Series Gran Turismo. Geometric structures that seem to grow from the car's body were covered in specially coloured Kvadrat fabrics by Ridolfo, and complemented by an array of innovative products that explore the theme of the car as an extension of the home.

Ronan & Erwan Bouroullec *Textile Field*
Created for the 2011 London Design Festival, *Textile Field* was first installed in the magnificent Raphael Gallery of the Victoria and Albert Museum. Measuring 30m × 8m and upholstered in 13 subtly gradated shades of *Hallingdal*, *Textile Field* creates a playful, comfortable and colourful environment in which visitors are invited to sit, stand or lie and contemplate their surroundings. *Textile Field* has since been installed at the Centre Pompidou – Metz, The Museum of Contemporary Art, Chicago, and Les Arts Décoratifs, Paris.

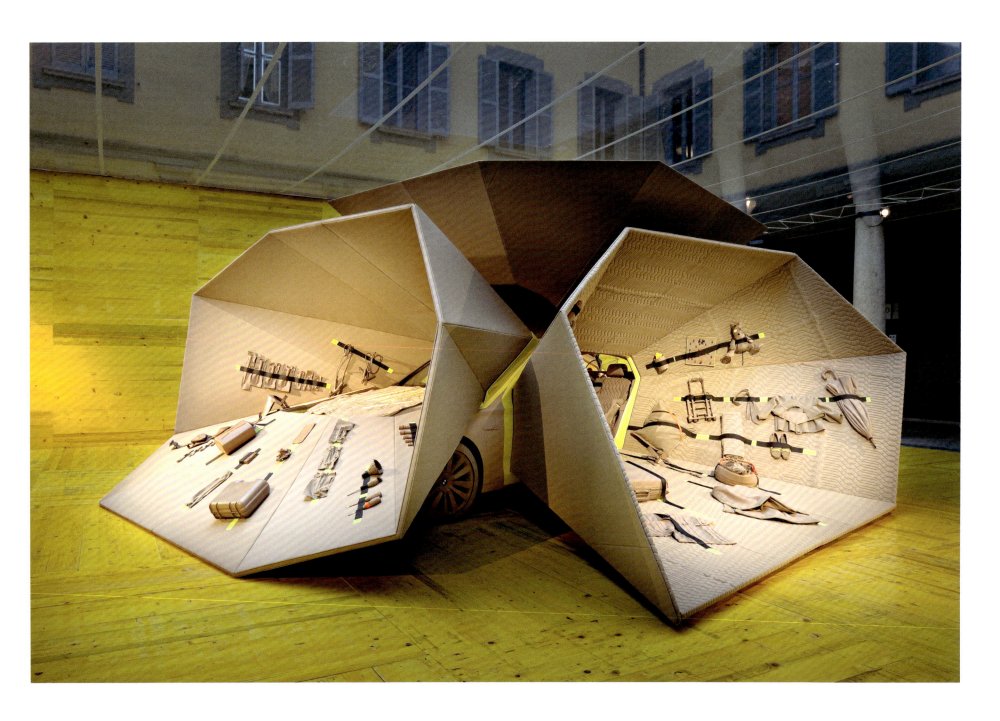

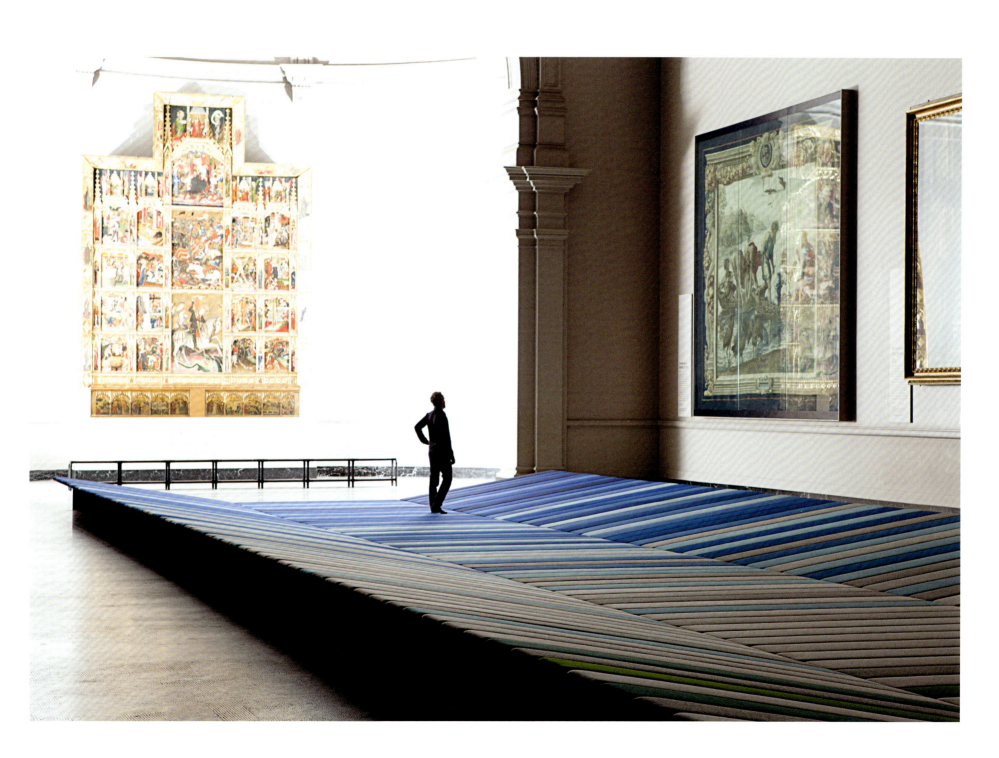

Olafur Eliasson and Kjetil Thorsen, *Serpentine Gallery Pavilion*, 2007 (London)

Jean Nouvel, *Serpentine Gallery Pavilion*, 2010 (London)

There's a notable sense of understatement about Kvadrat as a company – not false modesty, but rather Scandinavian reserve; warmth beneath the cold, as it were. And it does get pretty cold in Ebeltoft – on the east coast of Jutland, Denmark – in winter, though during the summer months it is very much a tourist destination, with people flocking to its elegant timber summerhouses and to the peninsula's beaches. Visiting Kvadrat's facilities is not like a tour of the usual industrial estates anyone involved in manufacture today might be familiar with. Arriving on site, visitors find themselves in a beautiful landscape once shaped by glaciers, beneath a vast open sky, staring at a clean, crisp modernist building emerging out of meadows rather than tarmac. When the artist Olafur Eliasson first visited in 2008, he was reminded of his childhood, as he recalls:

'My mother is a tailor, so as a child I occasionally went with her to companies who make fabrics. I have been to fabric fairs and companies where you walk through row upon row of fabrics. When I visited Kvadrat, that's what I was expecting: a dusty storage space with rolls and rolls of wool, and a forklift driving through the aisles. But when I got there, I was surprised to find that it was not dark. It was very bright inside and it was quiet. I thought I must

have arrived during a holiday because it was so incredibly quiet. I walked through the door and I stood there for a while until someone walked by – almost in slow motion, looking at me, and smiling. I asked myself, what is this place? Then suddenly, Anders Byriel, the CEO, came running out of his office, breaking the silence by calling out to welcome me. He took me round and it turned out that there were plenty of people hiding at their desks, but it was interesting that the ambience was very calm. And then after going around a few corners, I finally got into the fabric storage space with its endless metres of fabric, which I recognised. Even though I knew Kvadrat was a global company, it seemed as if I had come to a local business. It was only when I saw all the people wearing headsets that I realised they were actually connected to the outside world from this bright, quiet, local factory.'

'Our first idea was that our involvement in contemporary art should take the form of temporary projects, created for specific sites and museum shows,' says Anders Byriel. It was perhaps not surprising, therefore, that Kvadrat was asked to help with the 2007 *Serpentine Gallery Pavilion* in London's Kensington Gardens, designed by Olafur Eliasson and Norwegian architect Kjetil Thorsen. The

Serpentine Gallery annually presents a new pavilion around which to host many of their summer events and outreach programmes; it's one of the most ambitious temporary architectural projects in the world. Kvadrat provided the remarkable pavilion – which illuminated by night resembles anything from a hat or spinning top to a zoetrope or shark – with textiles and movable seating.

'I wanted to address the interior in a more tangible way, so it was natural … to reach out to Kvadrat because that is their focus,' explains Eliasson. 'We needed to work with someone who understood the importance of working creatively and who could react quickly. They made the balls, curtains and cushions, and also they assisted us in manufacturing. We selected the fabrics and colours for the light and texture – we needed an intense colour and exactly the right texture … These soft furnishings had an enormous effect on how people used the space because they invited people to play.'

This marked the start of Kvadrat's relationship with the Serpentine Gallery's pavilion programme; three years later they donated 220m of their textile *Blitz* to the bold and bright red pavilion designed by French architect Jean Nouvel. Kvadrat's collaborations often turn into ongoing relationships, and having worked on the 2007 pavilion, they have since got to know

Below and facing page: Olafur Eliasson and Kjetil Thorsen, *Serpentine Gallery Pavilion*, 2007 (London)

Life is space 4, 2012 (Studio Olafur Eliasson, Berlin)

Eliasson and his studio well. They have recently become involved in Eliasson's *Life is space* sessions in Berlin – a not-quite-annual get-together of artists, academics, dancers, theorists and anyone interested in uses of space. At *Life is space* in summer 2011, Kvadrat invited along a number of guests in order to build more bridges to the design world, including Peter Saville (who is a creative consultant to Kvadrat) and the design consultancy Graphic Thought Facility. Following the event, Saville and GTF produced a book about the project, which Kvadrat subsequently published. It was an experimental publication: no two copies were the same, with each containing images in different, random sequences.

Another collaboration with Eliasson has since been completed, resulting from his aforementioned visit to the Kvadrat complex back in 2008. Attracted to the landscape around Kvadrat's premises, Eliasson was invited to work on a project for the grounds with landscape architect Günther Vogt. For the resulting artwork, *Your glacial expectations*, Eliasson created five circular and elliptical mirrors, each of differing proportions and set in horizontal alignment in the landscape.

In close collaboration with Eliasson, Vogt worked on the landscape, creating oval groves of various sizes from different species of tree left to grow wild. The

trees – one species per grove – were chosen to reflect aspects of the landscape at different times of the year by means of coloured foliage, flowers and fruit. Set in grassy meadows grazed by Icelandic grey sheep, a mown path leads visitors between the mirrors and the trees, with a number of chairs dotted around the landscape for people to sit in and soak up the world around them. This poetic project, which will continue to evolve over time, marked a transition for Kvadrat from temporary site-specific works only to also being involved in longer-term and permanent pieces. It simultaneously (and inadvertently) transformed Kvadrat into a commissioner of contemporary art, beyond simply supporting projects by other organisations.

Art and design have been embedded in the corporate culture of Kvadrat since the company opened for business in 1968. Collaboration has always been a natural part of their process of developing products, but as is evident from their work with Olafur Eliasson, Kvadrat's relationship with art and design does not begin and end with product development for their own ranges; they use their facilities and expertise in the development and creation of new art, pushing the boundaries of exhibition design in the process. The experiences of working on such challenging projects inform the company's own research and development, making it a mutually

beneficial relationship – something that curator Hans Ulrich Obrist might describe as a 'feedback loop'.

Kvadrat's support of major art ventures began by happenstance in 2004 when the company agreed to help create Finnish designer Aamu Song's *Reddress*, first shown at the Louisiana Museum of Modern Art in Denmark the following year. Using over 550m of Kvadrat's *Divina* fabric, a vast red dress was fabricated, around 4m in height and 20m in diameter. The dress, which is now in the permanent collection of the Design Museum in Helsinki, serves as both an installation and performance space, with the dress being 'worn' by a performer who climbs in using a set of steps hidden inside. An audience of 238 people can be accommodated within the folds of the dress, enveloping them within the performance. The project has since been staged in several European cities, and in 2011 was presented at the London Design Festival. Kvadrat's first venture into contemporary art and design projects was thus not a strategic decision, but rather a response to a request for assistance.

A few months after Kvadrat's first collaboration on Song's *Reddress*, the company found itself involved in another out-of-the-ordinary project when it was approached by art gallery Sprüth Magers to help produce a new installation by German artist Rosemarie

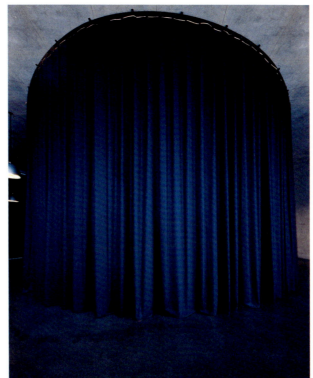

Thomas Demand, *Trick*, 2003 (Kunsthaus Bregenz, Austria)

Trockel for her mid-career retrospective at the Museum Ludwig in Cologne. Entitled *Yes, but*, the installation took the form of a vast curtain of woollen threads that visitors were invited to enter. Over a ton of white wool was used, with some parts dyed blood red and certain sections cut out like small dark tunnels. Within the context of the exhibition, which was entitled *Post-Meno-pause*, the installation created a womb-like experience. This imposing work, with its powerful (and undoubtedly, for some viewers, uncomfortable) subject matter, demonstrated Kvadrat's willingness not only to take on challenging production processes, but also to engage seriously with the critical discourse and visual languages of contemporary art. Through this project, it became clear that Kvadrat's nascent interest in art was not developing into the usual model of corporate arts patronage and sponsorship.[1]

Kvadrat's ongoing relationship with Thomas Demand began in 2003 when the artist was preparing for his first major museum show in Austria at the Kunsthaus Bregenz. Demand was keen to devise a moving curtain structure that would allow his film *Trick* to be presented in darkness whilst retaining a fluid relationship with the wider exhibition spaces.

A substantial pair of dark-blue curtains – around 70 m wide – was fabricated by Kvadrat in customised *Divina* upholstery fabric and installed on specially made tracks that enabled the curtains to spiral gradually into the centre of the room. The result was a space that became blacked out every 12 minutes, allowing just the right amount of time for viewers to be able to see the minute-long film.

While the curtain was not an artwork in itself, it initiated Kvadrat into the world of exhibition design whilst fuelling Demand's wider thinking about the presentation of his artworks. Clearly growing out of this collaboration, Kvadrat's second project with Demand took the relationship between his work and exhibition design to an entirely new level. For his first major solo show in Germany, at the Neue Nationalgalerie in Berlin in 2009, Kvadrat took on the immense task of providing 5 km of its *Tonica* fabric to divide up the space within the gallery and on which to present Demand's photographs. The Neue Nationalgalerie was designed by Mies van der Rohe and opened in 1968, and its spaces are both beautiful and unorthodox in terms of museum architecture, offering a challenging environment for the presentation of two-dimensional art. By means of a support structure that was hidden from view, Demand's photographs seemed to float against the heavy, custom-dyed grey-brown and green-gold curtains. Theatrical but understated, active yet passive, elegant yet utilitarian, the curtains created a unique exhibition experience.

'There wasn't a single wall I could use,' explains Demand. 'But I always find it a waste of resources to work against the existing architecture, so we were searching for some overlooked element that Mies had introduced and how we could make that into the main feature. Walls would always compete with the idea of the space, so to have erected walls would have looked like we didn't understand the proposition … The curtains did not necessarily affect the reading of single pictures but they dominated the nature of the show. There was no echo, for instance. The textiles muffled everything and somehow people were more alone within the space than usual – a very peculiar effect which obviously resonated well with the idea of memory.'

The exhibition was designed in collaboration with architects Caruso St John, who were conscious not only of the fact that Demand's exhibition exclusively featured works addressing events in Germany's history since 1945, but also that the timing of the exhibition coincided with both the sixtieth anniversary of the foundation of the Federal Republic of Germany and the twentieth anniversary of the fall of the Berlin Wall. In this context, the exhibition design resonated with

Above and facing page: Aamu Song, *Reddress*, 2004 (Louisiana Museum of Modern Art, Copenhagen)

themes of covering and uncovering, concealing and revealing, blocking and permitting, opening and closing, dividing and bringing together.[2]

In 2009 Kvadrat also supported the redevelopment of London's Whitechapel Gallery through a project with New York-based Liam Gillick – a British artist known for his collaborative and interdisciplinary approach to contemporary art, whether with artists, architects, designers or writers. His project involved selecting a spectrum of fabrics – in colours ranging from bright yellows to vivid blues and lime greens – to cover the chairs in the Whitechapel's new Zilkha auditorium. Entitled *Prototype Conference Room*, this strikingly colourful installation emphasised the unique identities of the individual members of an audience – whom it is perhaps easy to consider as an undifferentiated group when seated on uniformly coloured chairs – whilst simultaneously encouraging visitors actively to consider the designed environment around them.

That same year, Kvadrat invited Roman Signer to visit Ebeltoft with a view to commissioning a work from the artist to take place on site. After a week in Ebeltoft, Signer returned home and worked on some drawings. The process resulted in two works – *Tuch* and *Bogen* – that were staged on the nearby beach. A small yellow car arrived from Hamburg covered in warning signs –

it was full of Signer's signature explosives. 'I was a little concerned at first!' says Byriel. Using Kvadrat textiles, Signer created time-based works in which coloured fabrics were fired into the sky, briefly creating patterns in the air before falling to the ground: a project that took the medium of sculpture into the realms of the temporal and even ephemeral (not to mention into the domains of video and performance, too).

In 2011, Kvadrat collaborated for a third time with Thomas Demand, this time fabricating the work of art itself. In a remarkable site-specific piece for the Städel Museum in Frankfurt's grand and airy Metzler Hall, *Saal* involved a sophisticated trompe-l'oeil with a conceptual twist. Appearing to be a heavy crimson velvet curtain (replete with dense folds) covering all the hall's walls, in Demand's trademark style it was actually a photographic reproduction of curtains made out of paper, which were then printed on flat textiles. This subtle and decidedly postmodern artwork gave an impression of elegant simplicity that belied the complexity of both the concept and its execution – an aluminium frame system incorporating a spring mechanism was devised to support the panels. All of the measurements had to be absolutely perfect, or the illusion would have failed, with Kvadrat needing to match the meticulous attention to detail that Demand's

work involves. 'I had to devise something that wasn't too imposing but at the same time wasn't invisible,' Demand explains. 'And equally something that would be more than mere decoration. I found this both challenging and interesting ... I looked through their [the Museum's] collection of medieval art and was mesmerised by all the folding and drapery, and that was the starting point ... It was a complex project for me, and I don't think it was a straightforward project for Kvadrat.'

While curiosity, enjoyment and enthusiasm are clearly motivating forces, Kvadrat's art projects also showcase the skills, design, engineering, textile technology and manufacturing capabilities of the company. 'It is helping us to explore the technology that our company offers,' comments Byriel. For the opening of Kvadrat's Paris showroom in 2012, Swedish artist Miriam Bäckström developed the interactive artwork *See What You've Made Me Do*, using technology called *Luminous textile* that was developed by Philips in collaboration with Kvadrat Soft Cells. The technology is exciting – in essence an audio-visual fabric that uses multicoloured LEDs in combination with Kvadrat's acoustic *Soft Cells* panels, meaning that colour and moving imagery can be presented on textiles. Bäckström's project involves eight of these special rectangular textile panels arranged in an overlapping

abstract geometric configuration in one corner of the showroom. Combining to create a kind of 'machine', the panels respond to movement and sound in the space picked up by cameras and microphones. Clients and visitors can thus engage with the work, affecting what appears on screen. The interaction is made yet more complicated by software that both records and reconstitutes people's interaction, bringing an element of surprise and randomness to the process.

    Of the evolution of Kvadrat's art projects, Peter Saville says, 'Kvadrat is not part of some marketing strategy, deliberately making inroads into art to communicate their brand. That has not yet contaminated the way Kvadrat work and I hope it never will. They get more involved than that, supporting, developing and fabricating amazing things, and with a real spirit of liberal, creative endeavour.' It is equally clear the artists feel that they learn a lot from their collaboration with the company, and that it has affected their thinking and practice as a result. For his part, Thomas Demand commends both the company's respect and its shared sense of curiosity when engaging in art projects. 'It has opened up many interesting possibilities,' he comments. 'Fabric is nearly as ubiquitous as paper, and is as easily overlooked.'

1   Rosemarie Trockel's *Yes, but* is now scheduled to be in installed at the Kvadrat headquarters in Ebeltoft.
2   Following the collaboration with Thomas Demand in Bregenz, in 2008 Caruso St John approached Kvadrat to work with them to create the environment of the Frieze Art Fair in London: *Divina* was used to create the walls inside the tent. Caruso St John subsequently came to the idea of using the textile for the exhibition at the Neue Nationalgalerie. Kvadrat has maintained an ongoing relationship with Frieze since 2008.

Above and facing page: Roman Signer, *Tuch*, 2009 (Ebeltoft, Denmark)

Above and facing page: Roman Signer, *Bogen*, 2009 (Ebeltoft, Denmark)

Above and facing page: Rosemarie Trockel, *Yes, but*, 2005 (Museum Ludwig, Cologne)
Following page: Thomas Demand, *Saal*, 2011 (Städel Museum, Frankfurt)

Portfolio

Caruso St John with Thomas Demand, exhibition
design for Demand's major solo exhibition at the
Neue Nationalgalerie, Berlin (2009)

'There wasn't a single wall I could use. But I always
find it a waste of resources to work against the existing
architecture, so we were searching for some overlooked
element that Mies had introduced and how we could
make that into the main feature. Walls would always
compete with the idea of the space, so to have erected
walls would have looked as if we didn't understand the
proposition. Also, there were other associations in play,
like the silk and velvet cafe by Mies' partner Lilly Reich,
and how Helmut Kohl, the dominant political figure
in Germany over the last three decades, was married
to Hannelore Kohl, a woman who is said to have been
allergic to light. The official chancellor's residence in
Bonn is a beautiful and prestigious modernist pavilion
by Sep Ruf, which very much pays respect to Mies.
Hannelore Kohl had curtains installed immediately just
to be able to exist there. I kind of thought, if someone
were to reside in the Neue Nationalgalerie, 40 years
later there would surely be curtains by now to keep the
curious neighbours at bay. […] The curtains did not
necessarily affect the reading of single pictures but they
dominated the nature of the show. There was no echo,
for instance.

The textiles muffled everything and somehow people
were more alone within the space than usual – a very
peculiar effect which obviously resonated well with
the idea of memory. Interestingly, the show keeps
developing in people's memories: the feedback was
positive at the time, but now people are referring to
it as phenomenal!'

Thomas Demand

Olafur Eliasson   Grey sheep

Geneticists and sheep breeders today admire Icelandic sheep for their great diversity of colours and patterns. Traditionally, however, shepherds favoured white sheep because their wool could be easily dyed. Lambs with brown, black, patterned, or grey fleeces were slaughtered to maintain the 'purity' of the more marketable white flock. Breeding sheep for certain colours, however, can be quite challenging because dark-coloured lambs can be born to white ewes and vice versa – hence the proverbial 'black sheep', the odd family member who does not fit into the flock.

In Iceland, grey sheep especially were culled because they were difficult to find in the rocky terrain. Thus, grey sheep have become more and more scarce in Iceland over the generations. Olafur Eliasson is involved in an Icelandic initiative to reverse, through breeding, this age-old bias.

Icelandic grey sheep graze on a pasture in Ebeltoft, Denmark, as part of *Your glacial expectations*, a park designed by landscape architect Günther Vogt in collaboration with Eliasson for the Kvadrat head-quarters located there. Visitors (as well as the animals) will be reflected by five elliptical mirrors placed within the landscape. The mirrors' ovoid forms play with our expectations of a circle, creating a momentary illusion that causes us to renegotiate the space inside and outside the looking glass.

Similarly, shifting perspective was a recurring theme at *Life is Space 4*, a daylong, improvised exchange of ideas held at Studio Olafur Eliasson on 17 June 2011 with the support of Kvadrat. The event brought together an array of physicists, artists, musicians, dancers, architects, theoreticians, cooks, neuroscientists and students to share in a variety of experiments and presentations that ran the gamut of topics that occupy Eliasson and his studio: from compassion, black holes, cosmology and space and time, to movement, Chinese gardens, renewable energy and the function of memory. Throughout the day, a selection of artistic interventions and experiments – by students of the Institut für Raumexperimente and friends of Eliasson as well as by the artist himself – were on view in the studio and the adjoining *Grey sheep* space. *Grey sheep* is an ongoing project that expands the studio's activities by initiating a dialogue between artists associated with the house and a local audience.

Life is Space 4 fostered discussions among practitioners from various disciplines and backgrounds even after the official event closed; conversations continued over a shared meal of roast lamb prepared by Danish cook and slow-food activist Camilla Plum.

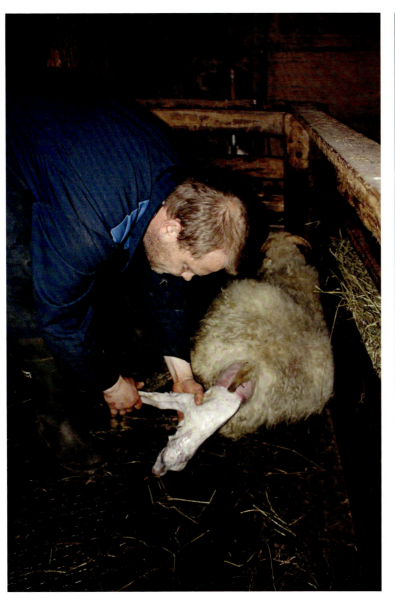
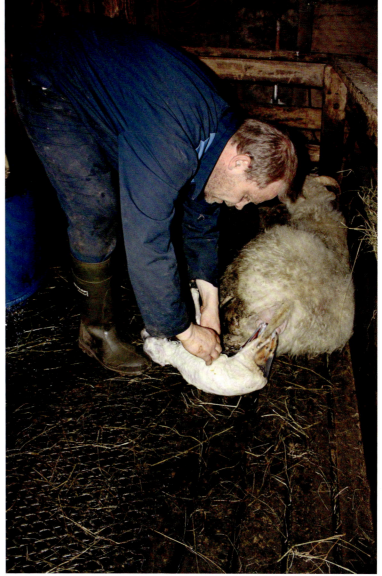

Peter Saville and Graphic Thought Facility

Peter and the sheep: the cover story

The book cloth used for this publication is a specially created prototype; a natural-toned woollen textile woven with randomly placed flashes of colour, making each cover a one-off. The development of the cloth and the creation of the book happened in parallel over a number of years. With the one illustrating the creative collaborations discussed in the other, they seemed natural partners.

A few years ago Anders Byriel invited Peter Saville, in his role as consultant to Kvadrat, to design a textile for the company. Inspired by flocks of sheep that he would see on trips back to his family home in North Wales, Peter suggested creating a design that married the grey and muddy natural tones of the winter fleeces to the lurid, almost DayGlo, tones of the sprays now used by shepherds in stock marking. Always attracted to sharp juxtapositions, Peter saw the brightly coloured stock markings as a kind of rural graffiti – an evocation of urban art in the middle of the countryside – and it was this 'punk pastoral' aesthetic that he wanted to bring to a fabric.

For Graphic Thought Facility to interpret Peter's proposal as an industrially produced textile, they needed to recapture the suggestion of unprocessed wool, complete with the apparently unwashed explosions of colour. It has been a complex process.

Weaving is a discipline born of – and constrained by – straight lines. To capture the haphazard dispersal and specific nature of this applied colour required a deep understanding of what was technically and creatively possible within these constraints. In the expanding circle of creative contacts drawn into this project GTF called upon the London-based weave designers Wallace Sewell.

Emma Sewell of Wallace Sewell liaised with mills, spinners and dyers to create a process and weave plan that would capture the essence of the marked wool, overseeing irregular dyeing techniques to mimic the piecemeal application of the stock marker sprays. The resulting textile changes constantly along its length – the wool apparently having been drawn raw from the sheep's backs and into the loom – giving every copy of this book a unique binding.

Kvadrat would like to thank:

Peter Saville for seeding the idea of a book some years ago, and for your contribution to its concept and art direction.

Robert Violette – who approached us at the kind recommendation of design gallerist Libby Sellers – and especially Hettie Judah of Violette Editions, for guiding and directing us, and for holding on to your beliefs while being open to our suggestions. You have created a wonderful publication with great contributors. It has been a pleasure working with both of you.

Andy Stevens and Robbie Mahoney of Graphic Thought Facility, for all your thoughts and for driving this project. We hope everybody will enjoy the visual journey you have created. Without you we would never have been able to realise this book.

Dr Denise Hagströmer, design historian and Senior Curator at The National Museum, Department of Design and Decorative Arts, Oslo, who has finally written down the Kvadrat story.

Jane Withers, a longtime friend and supporter, for her beautiful essay about colour since the 1960s.

Sevil Peach, for her inspiring and eye-opening essay on the use of textiles in modern architecture.

Tord Boontje, for sharing insights into his working methods with Hettie Judah and for allowing us to show the inspirations and sketches behind his products and his textiles for Kvadrat.

Ronan and Erwan Bouroullec for sharing their work and ideas, and to Zoë Ryan, curator of design at The Art Institute of Chicago, for communicating and contextualizing them.

Art photographer Joël Tettamanti, for his poetic documentation of production facilities and their surroundings in Britain and Switzerland.

Curator Matthew Price for his insightful essay on our involvement in art projects and work with artists.

Thomas Demand, for giving us the opportunity to collaborate, and for his continuous support, guidance and feedback.

Olafur Eliasson for his beautiful photographic essay about Icelandic grey sheep and the works they inspire. As part of *Your glacial expectations*, Icelandic grey sheep will soon graze on the meadows in Ebeltoft, Denmark.

Emma Sewell from Wallace Sewell who has, together with GTF, helped us to realise the book cloth.

Our colleague Njusja de Gier who, as managing editor of this book for Kvadrat, has guided it patiently and with great energy through the many stages in its long evolution.

We greatly appreciate the contributions of Giulio Ridolfo, Finn Sködt, Mathilde Aggebo, Julie Henriksen, David Nelson and Anne Jørgensen, who have been interviewed for several parts of this book. We are in particular grateful to Kirsten Toftegaard and Anja Lollesgaard of Designmuseum Danmark for their input in the historic part of this book, and to the art historian Vibeke Petersen. Thank you to Denni Ditzel and the Ditzel Estate, and to Jeppe Aagaard Andersen for permitting the use of archival images and textile samples. And to our Kvadrat colleagues Camilla Vissing Mogensen, Dorthe Aagaard Adamsen and Trine Hansen, who have been instrumental in sourcing images and checking facts.

A special thanks goes to the founders of Kvadrat, Poul Byriel and Erling Rasmussen, both for their participation and for starting this unique network of artists, designers and architects that has shaped Kvadrat. And to Mette Bendix and Anders Byriel for continuing to build and shape the company with their strong vision.

Kvadrat would never have become the company it is now without all the people that have worked and still are working for Kvadrat and all our friends, collaborators and supporters.

Last but not least, we want to thank Prestel, and Andrew Hansen in particular, for their enthusiasm in publishing the book that we felt was right for Kvadrat.

Aggebo and Henriksen: 99
Ole Akhøj: 43
Iwan Baan: 224, 254, 255
Courtesy BMW: 94, 95, 212, 213
Tord Boontje: 127, 130, 131, 132, 133, 141
© Wallace Collection, London, UK/The Bridgeman Art Library: 129
Studio Ronan & Erwan Bouroullec: 145–148, 154–156, 158–164, 216–218
© Thomas Demand/© COPYDAN, Kopenhagen 2013: 237–242
© Thomas Demand/© COPYDAN, Kopenhagen 2013. Photo © Nic Tenwiggenhorn. Courtesy Sprueth Magers Berlin London: 199, 225
© Thomas Demand/© COPYDAN, Kopenhagen 2013. Photo Norbert Miguletz: 234
© Rosemarie Trockel/© COPYDAN, Kopenhagen 2013: 232, 233
Suki Dhanda: 214, 215
Architekturfotografie Deimel + Wittmar. Courtesy Diener & Diener: 198

Studio Olafur Eliasson: 102, 104, 221, 245–253, 256–258
Annabel Elston: 8, 11–16, 120, 121 (right), 122
Luke Hayes: 223
Ole Hein Pedersen: 103
Roger Hiley: front cover
Mads Hjort (Hjortefar): 110, 111
Ariel Huber: 190, 192, 193
Morgane Le Gall: 152 (far left)
MGM/United Artists: 134
Angela Moore: 107, 109, 112–116, 121 (left), 123, 142
Moroso: 119
Courtesy Nanna Ditzel Design: 23, 25
Brahl Fotografi. Courtesy Nanna Ditzel Design: 87
K. Helmer-Petersen. Courtesy Nanna Ditzel Design: 22
John Offenbach: 222
© Panton Design, Basel: 27, 30 (left), 82 (right), 83, 84, 85, 152
Patricia Parineja: 210, 211
Poul lb Pedersen: 32, 33, 35, 37, 40
Thomas Pedersen: 32, 33
Raw-edges Design Studio: 108
Ed Reeves: 44, 100
Courtesy Peter Saville Studio: 101
Jean Prouvé © Scala, Florence/© ADAGP, Paris and DACS, London 2013: 154 (right)

©2013 DeAgostini Picture Library/Scala, Florence: 92
The Archive of Frank Stella, New York. © 2013. Photo Art Resource/Scala, Florence/© ARS, NY and DACS, London 2013: 82
Casper Sejersen: 42, 46, 86, 91, 96–98, 128, 157, 208–209
Courtesy Roman Signer: 228–231
Finn Sködt: 34
Ignazia Favata/Studio Joe Colombo, Milano: 152 (right)
Alex Sutton: 202 (right)
Hiroyuki Hirai. Courtesy Shigeru Ban Architects: 194, 196
Courtesy Aamu Song: 226
Courtesy Sou Fujimoto Architects: 195
Paul Tahon/Ronan & Erwan Bouroullec: 45, 93, 148, 150, 151
Joel Tettamanti: 140, 167–184, 205–207
Jørn Timm: 36 (left)
Gary Turnbull: 191, 202 (left)
UN Photo: 21
Courtesy Vitra: 41
Deidi von Schaewen: 187, 188, 189, 197

First published in 2013 by Prestel Verlag
in association with Violette Editions

© Kvadrat and Violette Limited, 2013
© for the photographs see page 263, 2013
© for the texts by the authors, 2013

Prestel, a member of
Verlagsgruppe Random House GmbH

Prestel Verlag
Neumarkter Strasse 28
81673 Munich
Tel +49 (0)89 4136-0
Fax +49 (0)89 4136-2335
www.prestel.de

Prestel Publishing Ltd.
14–17 Wells Street
London W1T 3PD
Tel +44 (0)20 7323 5004
Fax +44 (0)20 7323 0271

Prestel Publishing
900 Broadway, Suite 603
New York, NY 10003
Tel +1 (212) 995-2720
Fax +1 (212) 995-2733
www.prestel.com

Library of Congress Control Number: 2013943368

British Library Cataloguing-in-Publication Data:
a catalogue record for this book is available from
the British Library. The Deutsche Bibliothek
holds a record of this publication in the Deutsche
Nationalbibliografie; detailed bibliographical
data can be found under: http://dnb.d-nb.de

Prestel books are available worldwide. Please contact
your nearest bookseller or one of the above addresses
for information concerning your local distributor.

Kvadrat A/S
Lundbergsvej 10
8400 Ebeltoft
Denmark
www.kvadrat.dk

Originated and produced by Violette Editions
www.violetteeditions.com

Editorial direction: Hettie Judah and Robert Violette
Design and art direction: Graphic Thought Facility
Digital pre-press: Violette Editions
Copyediting and proofreading: Anna Blomefield
Picture research: Jo Walton, Isabella Kullmann
Printed in Italy

Verlagsgruppe Random House FSC® N001967
The FSC-certified paper Symbol™ Freelife™ has been
supplied by Fedrigoni Cartiere S.p.A., Verona, Italy
ISBN 978-3-7913-4858-2

431655